MANDELSLO'S TRAVELS IN WESTERN INDIA (A. D. 1638-9)

MANDELSLO'S TRAVELS IN WESTERN INDIA

(A. D. 1638-9)

BY

M. S. COMMISSARIAT, M.A.

Indian Educational Service; Professor of History and Political Economy, Gujarat College, Ahmadabad; Fellow of the University of Bombay

GYAN

Published by

Gyan Publishing House
5, Ansari Road
Daryaganj, New Delhi-110002
Phone: 011-47034999, 9811692060
E-mail: books@gyanbooks.com

Distribution Network
gyanbooks.com
India, USA, Canada, UK, Australia, France

ISBN : 978-81-212-3749-9 (PB)
First Published, 1931

2nd Impression 2020

Printed at: Gyan Press, Delhi.

Mandelslo's Travels in Western India
Author: M. S. Commissariat

MANDELSLO'S TRAVELS IN WESTERN INDIA

(A.D. 1638-9)

BY

M. S. COMMISSARIAT, M.A.

Indian Educational Service; Professor of History and Political Economy, Gujarat College, Ahmadabad; Fellow of the University of Bombay

HUMPHREY MILFORD
OXFORD UNIVERSITY PRESS
LONDON BOMBAY CALCUTTA MADRAS
1931

PREFACE

THE author owes a few words of explanation in presenting this little book to the public in the form in which it appears. The first English translation of Mandelslo's *Travels*, by J. Davies, was published in London, nearly three hundred years ago, in 1662, and the work is at present but little known and very rare. As the most valuable part of Mandelslo's *Travels* refers to his tour through Gujarat, I decided at first to give a critical summary of the same, with extracts, in my *History of Gujarat* which is in preparation. But when completed it was found that this account, in spite of my attempts at compression, extended over several chapters, and took up a rather disproportionate space in the larger historical work. It has, therefore, been decided to publish it as a separate book with the addition of chapters on Mandelslo's interesting visit to Goa, his account of the Portuguese in Western India and his return voyage to Europe.

Students of Indian history would naturally wish to see a new edition of the original English text of Mandelslo's work, and the firm of Routledge has already made arrangements for the publication of this text, in its excellent series of the 'Broadway Travellers', under the general editorship of Sir E. Denison Ross and Miss E. Power. But it is expected that the present work will supply a different want in its critical, historical and topographical remarks. As explained in the Introduction, it includes what is considered to be the original and authentic portion of Mandelslo's *Travels* which thus requires to be carefully examined. All that is first-hand and based on Mandelslo's personal experience and observation during the very few months that he was in India has been incorporated in this book.

My thanks are due to Principal H. G. Rawlinson, I.E.S., of the Deccan College, for his interest in this book, and to the Oxford University Press for valuable suggestions in its publication.

I hope that the map of Mandelslo's tour and the illustrations supplied will be appreciated by my readers, and I also trust that this little work will help to some extent to meet the interest, which I notice is every year on the increase, in the history of the province of Gujarat—a history which in the wealth of its materials and the variety and interest of its progress is perhaps unequalled by that of any other province in India.

M. S. COMMISSARIAT

Gujarat College, Ahmadabad

CONTENTS

APPENDIXES

LIST OF ILLUSTRATIONS

INTRODUCTION

JOHN ALBERT DE MANDELSLO was a young man of gentle birth attached as a page to the court of the Duke of Holstein, a small principality in the north of Germany. In 1635 the duke sent two ambassadors to the courts of Muscovy (Russia) and Persia on a commercial mission, and Mandelslo, then only twenty years old, was at his own request permitted to join them as an attaché. After sharing their adventures for three years, he parted company with them at Ispahan, in Persia, in 1638, being desirous of visiting India. Taking ship at the Persian Gulf, he arrived at Surat at the end of April 1638 and passed the whole of the rainy season there. In October he journeyed through the cities of Gujarat to the Mogul headquarters at Agra and Lahore. After a very brief stay at both these capital cities, he returned to the port of Surat, whence he sailed for England on 5 January 1639.

Adam Olearius, the secretary to the Duke of Holstein's embassy, was a learned person, being librarian and mathematician to the court, and he published in German, in 1646, an account of the adventures of the embassy in Russia and Persia under the title of *The Travels of the Ambassadors.* The work known to students of Indian history as Mandelslo's *Travels into the Indies* has, in some of its editions and translations, been given to the world as a supplement to Olearius' famous treatise and has been bound up with it as one volume. In this form it appears in the first English translation published in London by John Davies in 1662.

The credit to be given to the fairly voluminous production of Mandelslo has formed the subject of an interesting paper by the late Dr. Vincent A. Smith.[1] It is now clearly established that nearly two-thirds of the work which goes under his name is the contribution of the erudite Olearius and of his French translator, A. de Wicquefort. Mandelslo never went further east than India and yet the published versions of his voyages give long accounts of Sumatra, Java, the Moluccas, Japan and China, none of which countries was ever visited by him. He was also no scholar and yet his account of his tour in India is full of elaborate dissertations on the political, religious and social conditions of the people. Many of these interpolations are due to the pen of Olearius, to whom Mandelslo had entrusted his scanty narrative with an injunction that, if it was published, his friend 'would rather regard therein his reputation after his death than the friendship they had promised one another'. The French translator went even further and made large additions based on works of eastern travels available to him.

But while admitting this, no one who has perused the work that goes under Mandelslo's

[1] 'The Credit due to Mandelslo' in *The Journal of the Royal Asiatic Society* (1915), pp. 245–54.

name[1] can possibly deny that, so far as his stay at Surat and his tour through the cities of Gujarat in October 1638 are concerned, his record is based on his own personal observations and experiences, for he actually passed through the places which he describes and enjoyed the hospitality of both the English and Dutch merchants resident there. This part of his narrative bears all the impress of veracity and, when he is not an eye-witness, he takes care to tell us that his information was given to him by others during the journey.

The preface written by Olearius to his German edition of *Mandelslo's Travels* has been utilized, but not fully reproduced, by John Davies in his English version. But we find it printed *in extenso* in the French translation published by de Wicquefort.[2] From this we obtain some very useful information about the history of our author's manuscript. We are told that, on his return to Surat from his tour in Gujarat, Mandelso made a sort of literary testament so far as his journal was concerned. This was dated Surat, 25 December 1638, a few days before his ship, the *Mary*, left Suvali bar on her

[1] 'The Travels of J. Albert de Mandelslo into the East Indies' in Olearius' *Voyages and Travels of the Ambassadors*, translated into English by John Davies, London (1662).

[2] The first edition of the French translation of Mandelslo's *Travels* was published by Abraham de Wicquefort in 1662. The library of the Bombay Branch of the Royal Asiatic Society possesses a valuable copy of a later French reprint of the same entitled: *Voyages célèbres et remarquables faits de Perse aux Indes Orientales par le Sr. Jean-Albert de Mandelslo*, published in folio at Amsterdam in 1727.

return voyage to Europe. With the perils of a long sea voyage before him, Mandelslo says:

'As all this has been written in haste and without order, and noted only from my memory, and as I had not the time while travelling to put it in the required form, I warn and request my friends, in whose hands it may fall after my death, not to publish it lest people should take the occasion to criticize it. But if my friends think it worth publishing for the sake of commemorating my name, I desire them to entrust this work to Sieur Olearius, who was my friend and companion for four years, and who may be found at Leipzic or at Reval or in Livonia. Let them request him on my behalf either to make a summary or to prepare an entire narrative of my travels to the memory of his dear friend and faithful companion who has finished his days in travelling, not to derive any gain from the same, but for the good of the public and his own pleasure. . . . Written at Surat, 25 December 1638.'

In a postscript to the above, Mandelslo adds that if Olearius could not be found, his friends might entrust the work to some other capable person; and further expresses his desire that, as His Highness the Duke of Holstein-Gottorp had not only given him the opportunity of undertaking his travels, but also furnished him with the means of completing them, the work might be dedicated to this prince, 'the Maecenas of scholars,' as a mark of the gratitude of the author for the favours received by him.

Mandelslo, having happily returned to his native country from his travels in May 1640, had an interview with Olearius on the subject of the editing of his itinerary, and it was then decided that he should rewrite it and put it in order. Thereafter he entered the service of the King of France as a Captain of Cavalry under M. Josias de Rantzau, Marshal of France, who was himself a native of Holstein. Unfortunately, Mandelslo was destined to be cut off in the prime of life, for, during a visit to Paris soon after, he fell a victim to smallpox, then one of the scourges of Europe.

After his untimely death, the manuscript of his itinerary was found among his effects by his sister Madam Lucy Catherine *née* de Mandelslo, widow of the Lord of Schulenbourg. She decided, as a pious duty, to publish this 'curious and useful' work of her brother and with this object she approached Olearius and asked him to undertake it, reminding him of her brother's last wishes in regard to the manuscript. At the same time, she advanced him several hundred crowns to meet the expenses of the publication in order that the work might be completed promptly and without delay. Mandelslo's narrative was published in German by Olearius at Schleswig in 1658 with a great many additions and embellishments. According to the author's wishes, it was dedicated to Frederick, Duke of Schleswig, of Holstein, of Ditmarsh, Count of Oldenburg and Delmenhorst, and to 'his illustrious wife' Marie Elizabeth, of the Electoral House of Saxony. The dedication was made on the duke's sixtieth birthday, on 22 December 1657.

To Mandelslo's sister then and to his trusted friend Olearius is posterity indebted for preserving for it a record of his journal. We have already referred above to the importance and value of his work so far as his travels in Gujarat are concerned, as being an original account based on personal observations. The same may be said to be true in connexion with the narrative of his visit to Goa on the west coast of India, where the *Mary*, which carried our author as well as William Methwold, the President of the Surat factory, halted for ten days to enable the latter to settle outstanding financial matters with the Portuguese authorities. Mandelslo's account of the visit to the Viceroy of Goa, of the great religious establishments and churches of the Jesuits and of the royal hospital in this city, is also first-hand, and we have, therefore, given elaborate extracts from the same. The more general account of the Portuguese in western India, which follows the above, contains probably much embellishment on the part of Olearius, though it is impossible to distinguish the editor's contribution from the original nucleus supplied by our author. It will not be denied, however, that the chapters devoted by us to Goa and the Portuguese in this book add to and supplement the information which is already available to us in the works of Linschoten, Pyrard de Laval, P. Della Valle and Dr. John Fryer. In order to complete our survey of Mandelslo's travels, the last two chapters of this work have been reserved for a rapid sketch of his return voyage to Europe, his stay in England and his journey through the Netherlands, till he reached his native town of Gottorp in Holstein on 1 May 1640.

An attempt has been made throughout this book to indicate, wherever possible, the various digressions or additions made by Mandelslo's German or French editors, for these have been responsible for the misunderstandings current among scholars about the 'credibility' of our traveller. The perusal of this book will, it is hoped, make it clear that it is not quite correct to say, as the late Dr. Vincent Smith has done, that 'Mandelslo's bubble reputation has been pricked beyond the possibility of repair'. It is true, indeed, that Mandelslo did not write the voluminous work which goes under the name of his *Travels into the Indies* and also that he never visited those far-eastern countries from Ceylon to China, the accounts of which cover no less than 128 closely printed folio pages in the first English edition of 1662. But we are entitled to say that, after all these extensive additions or interpolations have been carefully eliminated, a very respectable residuum remains which is purely his original composition, and which entitles him to a high rank among those travellers whose itinerary was confined to a somewhat narrow region of the Indian peninsula.

We must also be careful to note that, though the elaborate additions mentioned above are not from

Mandelslo's pen, they have nevertheless a historical importance of their own, for the information given in them is based on the best books on eastern travels available to Olearius or to de Wicquefort in the middle of the seventeenth century. By far the largest portion of the digressions refers to the lands of the Far East and to the peoples and places on the African coast. These accounts, therefore, deserve to be compared with others in order to form an estimate of their value; and to reject them summarily as interpolations and, therefore, of no value would be a strangely narrow attitude to take up in connexion with the use that can be made of this material.

THE

Voyages & Travels

OF

J. ALBERT de MANDELSLO

(A *Gentleman* belonging to the *Embassy*, sent by the Duke of HOLSTEIN to the great Duke of MUSCOVY, and the King of PERSIA)

Into the

East-Indies.

Begun in the year M. DC. XXXVIII. and finish'd in M. DC. XL.

Containing a particular description of

The great MOGUL's Empire, the Kingdoms of DECAN, CALICUTH, COCHIM, ZEILON, COROMANDEL, PEGU, SIAM, CAMBOLIA, MALACCA, SUMMATRA, JAVA, AMBOINA, BANDA, The MOLUCCAS, PHILIPPINE and other Islands, JAPAN, the Great Kingdom of CHINA, the Cape of GOOD HOPE, MADAGASCAR, &c.

In three Books.

Illustrated with Maps and Figures.

Rendred into *English*, by *JOHN DAVIES* of *Kidwelly*.

LONDON,

Printed for *Tho. Dring*, and *J. Starkey*, at the *George* in *Fleet-street*, near *Cliffords Inne*, and at the *Mitre* between the *middle-Temple gate*, and *Temple-Barre*.

M. DC. LXII.

FACSIMILE OF THE TITLE PAGE OF 'MANDELSLO'S TRAVELS'

PREFACE TO THE ENGLISH EDITION OF 1662

WE give below an extract from the Preface written by John Davies, of Kidwelly, to his English translation (from the French) of Olearius' *Voyages and Travels of the Ambassadors* published in London in 1662.

'TO THE READER,

'Mandelslo, a Gentleman well born, had his education at the Duke of Holstein's Court, to whom he had been a Page. Hearing of an Embassy intended for Muscovy and Persia, he would needs be one in it; and, as if he were that Virtuous Man who looks upon the whole World as his Country, he would not depart, ere he had obtained his Prince's leave, to see the other parts of Asia. During his abode at Ispahan he got acquainted with some English merchants who, speaking to him of the Indies, rais'd in him a desire to go thither. The King of Persia, to engage his stay at his Court, proffers him a Pension of Ten Thousand Crowns; he slights the favour of so great a Prince, gets on horseback, with no great sums about him, and sets forward on his Journey with a retinue of three German servants and one Persian who was to be his Guide and Interpreter but forsook him when he stood in most need of his service and assistance. It was also a very strange Adventure which made him find civil entertainment and hospitality at Surat; made him subsist at the charge of others; conducted him by Land to the Great Mogul's Court; brought him safely back again to Surat; preserv'd the ship he was in after so many tempests near the Cape of Good Hope; and miraculously delivered him, at his first arrival into England, when he was given over for irrecoverably lost in the very haven as may be seen near the end of his Travels.

'To these Mandelslo had a particular inclination and knew so well how to make his advantages thereof that Olearius himself makes no difficulty to confess that he met with, in his Notes, many things which might have been added to his Relation and have found a kind reception even among the more curious had he been as forward to have his Travels published as he had been to prosecute them. But Mandelslo, instead of giving the world that satisfaction and continuing with his friend who might have further'd him in his design, left the Court of Holstein, where he found not employment proportionate to his merit, and betaking himself to another Profession he got into a Regiment of horse commanded by a German who purely by his Military accomplishments had rais'd himself to one of the greatest dignities of France. He had therein the Command of a Troop and, being a person of much courage and endu'd with all the qualities requisite to the making up of a great man, was likely to have rais'd himself to a more than ordinary fortune when coming to Paris, to pass away the Winter, he there died of the smallpox.

'Being at Surat, in December 1638, he made a kind of Will concerning his Papers, which he put before the beginning of his Relation, wherein he desir'd his Friend Olearius not to suffer it to be publish'd in regard he had not had the leisure to digest it into order, or, if he did, that he would rather regard therein his reputation after his death than the friendship they had mutually promis'd one another and faithfully improv'd during the four years of their joint Travels.

'Mandelslo was no great scholar but could make a shift to understand a Latin Author which help'd him much in the attaining of the Turkish Language wherein he came to a considerable perfection. His Friend taught him also the use of the Astrolabe, so that he was able to take the Longitudes and Latitudes that are in several places of his Book and without which it had been impossible for him to be much skill'd in Geography, which makes the most considerable part of this kind of Relations.

'Olearius hath indeed been very much his Friend, not only in reforming and refining his Style which could not be very elegant in a person of his Profession, but also in making several observations and additions thereto, printing it in Folio in a very fair character, and adorning it with several pieces of Sculpture.

'Olearius's kindness to his Friend, in enriching his Relation with many excellent remarks, taken out of Emanuel Osorio,[1] Maffaeus,[2] and the chief Voyages of the Dutch, gave the French Translator thereof, A. de Wicquefort, occasion to augment the said Book with whatever he found excellent in all those who have given the best account of the East Indies. So that it is to him we are obliged for the exact description of the Province of Guzuratta, the Kingdom of Pegu, and Siam, etc., the state of the affairs of Zeilon, Sumatra, Java, the Moluccas and Japan, as also for the Religions of these Peoples. So that there is, in this Edition of ours, especially as to the Travels of Mandelslo, a third part more than there is in the largest of the German Editions.

'The Reader will find therein many things which will haply seem incredible to him; as, among others, he may haply be astonish'd at the wealth of a Governor of Amadabath, and at that of a King of Indosthan, as also at the vast revenues of the Provinces and Lords of China and Japan; but besides that there is nothing of Romance in all this, and that there is no comparison to be made between the wealth of Europe and that of Asia, there are many persons, in France and England, that will justify our Relation, though it said much more than it does.'

[1] *De Rebus Emmanuelis Lusitaniae regis virtute et auspiciis gestis, a Hieronymo Osorio*, Lisbon (1575). Jeronymo Osorio (1506–80) was a famous Portuguese prelate, historian and critic who acquired a European reputation by his works in Latin. The perfection of his prose style caused him to be named by contemporaries 'the Portuguese Cicero'.

[2] *Joan. Petri Maffeii Historiarum Indicarum*, Libri XVI, Cologne (1590).

CHAPTER I

MANDELSLO'S STAY AT SURAT

(APRIL TO SEPTEMBER 1638)

ON 6 April 1638 Mandelslo embarked at Gombroon (Bandar Abbas), in the Persian Gulf, on a small English ship, called the *Swan*, of 300 tons' displacement and carrying twenty-four guns. The English agent at Ispahan had given special instructions to the captain to conduct his distinguished passenger to Surat and to defray all his charges, and four guns were fired in Mandelslo's honour when he boarded the vessel, accompanied by several European and Indian merchants whose acquaintance he had made at the Persian port, and who came to see him off. The voyage to Surat occupied nineteen days, during which the captain honoured his guest by resigning his own bed in his favour and giving him precedence on all occasions. Mandelslo had suffered much in health during his journeys in Persia, and soon found himself considerably benefited by the excellent fare provided in the ship along with good sack, English beer, French wines, arrack and other cordials. He specially mentions the use of tea (described as *Thé*), which he took twice or thrice a day, as an important contributory factor in the recovery of his health.[1]

Embarks at Bandar Abbas for Surat

[1] J. Ovington, who was chaplain of the English factory at Surat in 1692-3, says that this drink was in common use in India in his time as a

This was the period when this famous beverage was gradually making its way among the upper classes in western Asia and Europe.

Searched at custom-house

The *Swan* reached Surat bar on 25 April, and four days later Mandelslo took leave of the captain and set out from Suwali for the ten miles' journey to Surat, in company of two English merchants who had been specially sent down to the coast by the President to receive him. Proceeding by boat up the Tapti river, with the prospect of a fertile soil, fair gardens and pleasant country-houses on both sides, the party landed not far from the Mogul governor's palace. They next proceeded to the custom-house, to have their effects searched by the officers there, 'which is done with such exactness in this place that they think it not enough to open chests and portmantles, but examine peoples' clothes and pockets'.[1] It was the practice for the governor of the city to make the passengers or merchants coming from

'healthful' beverage: 'Tea, with some hot spice intermixt and boiled in the water, has the repute of prevailing against the headache, gravel and griping in the guts, and 'tis generally drunk in India, either with sugar-candy, or, by the more curious, with small conserved lemons.'—J. Ovington, *Voyage to Surat*, edited by H. G. Rawlinson, p. 181.

[1] Sir Thomas Roe, who arrived at Surat at the end of 1615 as ambassador for King James to the court of the great Mogul, had to oppose a similar demand. The officials who were escorting him from the port of Suwali to the city claimed the right to search the persons of the members of his suite, though he himself was exempted by virtue of his high position. The following extract from the entry made by Roe in his journal is interesting:

'Then they began a new tune, that I would be pleased to be content that all my company might be searched, according to the custom of the country. I replied that I was the Ambassador of a mighty and free

foreign ports part with any commodity for which he took a fancy at the price which he thought fit to put upon it. On this occasion also, we are told that the governor came to the custom-house as soon as Mandelslo had reached it and, in spite of the young German's protests, he persisted in taking away a bracelet of yellow amber which he found in the baggage, promising to return it later.

He becomes the guest of the English factory

Leaving the governor to enjoy this rarity, Mandelslo entered an Indian coach, drawn by two white oxen, which the English President had sent to bring him to his house. Methwold was the head of the factory at this period and received the traveller with great kindness, his knowledge of Dutch helping to make the conversation easy. He told his guest that, as the rains would be setting in, no more ships were expected to arrive from Europe and that Mandelslo would have to postpone his intention of returning to Germany until the fair season. He promised, however, that if his guest would stay with him for five or six months, he would do all he could for his diversion and make arrangements for him to visit the most famous places in the country. Mandelslo gratefully accepted this advice and offer

Prince : that I would never dishonour my Master so much, whose Person I bare, as to subject myself to so much slavery: I would engage my Honour (which I esteemed as my life) that no follower of mine had the worth of a *Pice* of trade or merchandise : and that in Europe and most parts of Asia all Ambassadors and their trains were so far privileged as not to be subject to common and barbarous usage.'—*The Embassy of Sir Thomas Roe to India*, edited by Wm. Foster, Hakluyt Society, vol. I, pp. 47–48.

and, having been shown all over the house, he selected for himself a chamber adjoining that of the senior officer after the President, who was known as his second. In the evening, several of the English factors came to convey him to the supper-hall, where were assembled the minister to the factory with about a dozen merchants. They all sat down to dinner, with the exception of the President and his second, and were served with about fifteen or sixteen dishes of meat, besides the dessert.[1] When this was over, the chaplain took the visitor to a great open terrace, or gallery, where sat every night the President, his second, the principal merchant, the minister and Mandelslo to enjoy the cool breezes from the sea. The other factors did not attend unless specially invited by the President.

An account of the life of the English merchants

Mandelslo lays special stress on the great respect in which the President was held by everyone in the English house at Surat, and the order and regularity that prevailed in all matters. Divine service was held twice a day, at six in the morning and at eight o'clock at night. On Sundays, service was held three times. Everyone had his particular duties assigned to him and his hours fixed both for work and for recreation. A special function is men-

[1] Ovington, in his *Voyage to Surat* (pp. 230–1) gives a long and interesting account of the 'public' table at the English Factory, when all the factors sat down with the President and Senior Merchants, and dined off dishes of pure, massive silver, containing viands prepared by three different cooks—English, Portuguese and Indian—and drank the most expensive wines from Europe

tioned by Mandelslo, which illustrates the home longings which those early English merchants settled in India must have felt in days when it took nearly a year to receive news from the mother country. On every Friday, after prayers, a meeting took place, attended by the President and three other merchants who were related to him and who had all left their wives in England. This day of the week being that of their departure from England, they had appointed it as a commemoration day on which they drank their wives' healths. Mandelslo was invited to join these select meetings and tells us that some of the merchants took advantage of them to drink more than they could well carry, probably to drown their regrets.

Their diversions at Surat

The English at Surat owned a fair garden outside the town, to which all the factors resorted on Sundays after the sermon and sometimes on other days of the week. It is probable that the whole day was spent in this garden in various enjoyments. One of these was shooting at butts or targets, at which Mandelslo showed himself so expert that he was able to pocket a hundred *mahmudis*, or five pounds sterling, every week. This was followed by a collation of fruit and preserves, after which they bathed in a tank, or cistern, with water in it five feet deep, when some Dutch gentlewomen 'served and entertained them with much civility'. Mandelslo's very limited knowledge of the English tongue, however, prevented him from enjoying the full pleasure of these picnics, for he could converse freely only with the President who knew Dutch.

In a short account of the Mogul Empire and of its provinces which Olearius gives for the benefit of his readers at this stage in the travels, we are told that the province of Gujarat was improperly called by the Portuguese the 'Kingdom of Cambay' from its chief city where they had their principal trading and that it was 'without all question the noblest and most powerful of all the Mogul's country.' 'There is no province in all the Indies,' he adds, 'more fertile than Gujarat, nor any that affords more fruits and provisions which grow in such abundance there that all the neighbouring provinces are thence supplied'.[1]

Gujarat, the noblest province of the Mogul Empire

One of the most important historical references made by Mandelslo is where he mentions the terrible Gujarat famine of 1630–1, which was long remembered in the province as the *satyasio kal*.[2] It must be regarded as a conclusive proof of the credibility of our traveller and his exact information so far as

Reference to great famine of 1630-1

[1] Mandelslo, *Travels*, London (1662) pp. 20–22.

[2] Very full and graphic accounts of this terrible calamity which desolated the province of Gujarat, plunged some of its people into cannibalism, and set back production for a whole decade, are available in a number of contemporary works. See Peter Mundy, *Travels in India*, Hakluyt Society, vol. II, pp. 43, 44, 262, 265, 266, 275, 276; *English Factories in India*, edited by Foster, 1630–3; Elliot and Dowson, *History of India*, vol. VII, p. 24; and the account of the Dutch merchant, van Twist, in Moreland, *From Akbar to Aurangazib*, pp. 21–23.

An exhaustive chapter has been devoted to this subject in the author's *History of Gujarat* which is in preparation.

this province is concerned. When writing of the fertility of Gujarat and the abundance of provisions which it supplied at the time, he is reminded of the grievous calamity through which the country had passed some years before his arrival. His remarks deserve to be quoted:

'It is true, indeed, that in the year 1630 the great drought and the year following the continued rains reduced it to so deplorable a condition that the particular accompt (that) might be given thereof would deprive the Reader of the diversion which it is our design to find him in this Relation. But the province hath since that time well recovered itself of that desolation, yet not so as but the marks of it may be seen everywhere'.[1]

Visit to Rander, Damri and other villages

In June 1638, Mandelslo went out hunting with a young Dutch merchant and another who was an Englishman, and crossing the river arrived at Rander[2] which he describes at this early period as an old ruined city where the Dutch had a warehouse. The inhabitants whom he calls Naites (Navayats)[3] were either mariners or tradesmen professing the Muslim reli-

[1] Mandelslo, op. cit., p. 22.

[2] Rander, situated on the right bank of the Tapti, about two miles above Surat, is admitted to be one of the oldest cities in southern Gujarat. In 1530, Rander was sacked and burned by the Portuguese general, Antonio da Silveira, after a brave but unavailing defence by its warlike Moslem population. The town never recovered from this blow, while Surat, which had also been plundered, recovered and soon took the place of its rival.—*Bombay Gazetteer*, vol. II, pp. 299, 300 and *n*.

[3] Navayat is probably derived from the Sanskrit *nava-ayata* meaning 'new-comers'. From the first quarter of the thirteenth century, the ancient

gion. At the village of Damri he drank of some toddy or palm-wine in the orthodox fashion in cups made of leaves. The method of extracting the liquid from the trees is the same to-day as it was three hundred years ago. 'To get out the juice,' says our traveller, 'they go up the top of the tree, where they make an incision in the bark and fasten under it an earthen pot which they leave there all night, in which time it is filled with a certain sweet liquor very pleasant to the taste. They get out some also in the day time, but that corrupts immediately and is good only for vinegar which is all the use they make of it.'[1]

Surat described: Its gates, houses and port

Mandelslo next turns to describe the city of Surat in which he stayed for fully five months before proceeding on his tour to the north at the end of the rainy season. The town had three gates, one of which led to Cambay and Ahmadabad after crossing the river, the second led to Burhanpur, and the third to Navsari. The entrance to the castle had a spacious *maidan* in front of it. Near by were the governor's palace and the custom-house and adjoin-

town of Rander had been dominated by a race of foreign Muhammadans who were called Navayats. These immigrants were Arabs from Kufa, who, being Shiahs, were persecuted by the orthodox Sunnis, and fled from their native country to India where they settled at various places on the west coast. According to tradition they overpowered the Jain population of Rander and became its rulers. Being active navigators they became in course of time wealthy and successful merchants. The Navayats have long ceased to be of importance at Rander and their place as traders has been taken by Bohras of the Sunni sect.—*The Book of Duarte Barbosa*, edited by Dames, vol. I, pp. 146, 147 and *n*.

[1] Mandelslo, op. cit., p. 23.

ing these was the bazaar for foreign as well as local merchants. The Mogul governor in charge of the castle was independent of that of the city. It was the business of the latter to administer justice and look after the customs on goods exported and imported. The duty was three and a half per cent *ad valorem* on all commodities, except on gold and silver, whether in coins or in bars, which paid two per cent only. The spacious and well-built houses belonging to the Dutch and English companies were called lodges. The harbour of Surat was at the village of Suwali, where foreign ships unloaded, the goods being then conveyed to the city by land. 'It is very safe riding,' says Mandelslo of Suwali bar, 'there being no danger of any wind but that of the south-west. But from May to September, there is no staying on those coasts, by reason of the winds and tempests, accompany'd by extraordinary thunder and lightning which reign there during all that time."[1]

The Moslem inhabitants

In his description of the population of Surat, Mandelslo says that the Moguls in the city were looked upon with more respect than were the Banyas or Brahmins because of their religion which was that professed by the Great Mogul himself, as also on account of their capacity to bear arms. They had, however, an aversion to trade and business and preferred service to any honourable profession, 'for if they can but once get to be masters of a horse they court fortune

[1] Mandelslo, op. cit., p. 23.

no further and immediately lift themselves in the service of their Prince.'[1] The Banyas, on the other hand, were a hard-working class, attached to trade and merchandise, with an extraordinary devotion towards religious matters.

Surat, the headquarters of English trade

Among the foreigners resident at Surat were Arabs, Persians, Armenians, Turks and Jews, but none of these classes had such large and wealthy settlements as had the Dutch and the English settled at Surat. These two nations had their lodges, their store-houses, their presidents, their merchants and their secretaries, so that they made the place 'one of the most eminent cities for traffic of all the East'. Surat was in particular the headquarters of all the English factories throughout the Indies. The President managed the affairs of the East India Company with the help of twenty or twenty-four merchants and officers, and had under his superintendence the factories at Agra, Ispahan, Masulipatam, Cambay, Ahmadabad, Baroda, Broach, and Dabul in the Konkan. The secretaries in charge of these subordinate factories had to come once in a year to Surat and give an account of their administration to the President. The factory at Bantam in the isle of Java had no doubt its own President, who had no dependence on that of Surat. But even he observed a certain deference towards the latter, and so did the captains of all the English ships coming to the east, for no ship would consider

[1] Mandelslo, op. cit., p. 24.

its voyage complete until it had cast anchor at Surat.

After declaring that 'the places about this city are the most delightful of any in the world',

The famous Gopi Talav

Mandelslo refers to a tank or cistern 'made eight square of freestone', which was evidently the famous Gopi Talav. It was so spacious that it contained enough water to supply the whole city even in the hottest months of the year. The tank had at every angle a series of steps leading to the water and in its centre stood a pleasure house which the traveller describes as the 'tomb' of the builder of this magnificent structure.[1]

In the middle of September, news came of the arrival of two English ships at Suwali bar and as

Arrival of ships from Europe

the President had some business of importance with the governor, he sent two of the leading merchants along with Mandelslo to give them a welcome. They were all treated hospitably on both the vessels and on the first day of their arrival the better part of the night was spent in obtaining news of the affairs of Europe. When the President reached Suwali after about eight days, the two commanders of the ships and the others went out to honour him, at which interview the latter 'made a short discourse to them, exhorting them to show their fidelity and compliance

[1] For the history of the Gopi Talav see *Bombay Gazetteer*, vol. II, p. 312, 'Surat and Broach'. It was constructed in the early part of the sixteenth century by a Brahmin, named Malik Gopi, who was a high officer of Sultan Muzaffar II of Gujarat (1511–25). Malik Gopi is described by the Portuguese as Lord of Surat and Broach.—*Travels of P. Della Valle*, vol. I, p. 34 and n.

to their superiors during the time they should stay in the Indies.' On the President next proceeding to one of the ships, he was received with a salute of twelve guns, and subsequently on going to the other they fired sixteen guns.

Mandelslo leaves Surat for Ahmadabad

Though the rainy season was now over, Mandelslo was informed that the English ships in which he proposed to return to Europe would not be ready for departure in less than three or four months. He therefore accepted the advice of the President to join a caravan that was proceeding to Ahmadabad and thus acquaint himself with the Mogul's country. His stay of five months at Surat with the English factors had proved a very enjoyable one and he says that he 'wanted for no divertisment'. The Dutch President at Surat had his family with him and the German traveller spent much time with them, especially because he could converse there in his own tongue.[1]

[1] The chief of the Dutch factory in Surat at this period was Barent Pieterszoon.—*English Factories* (1637-41) edited by W. Foster, p. 240.

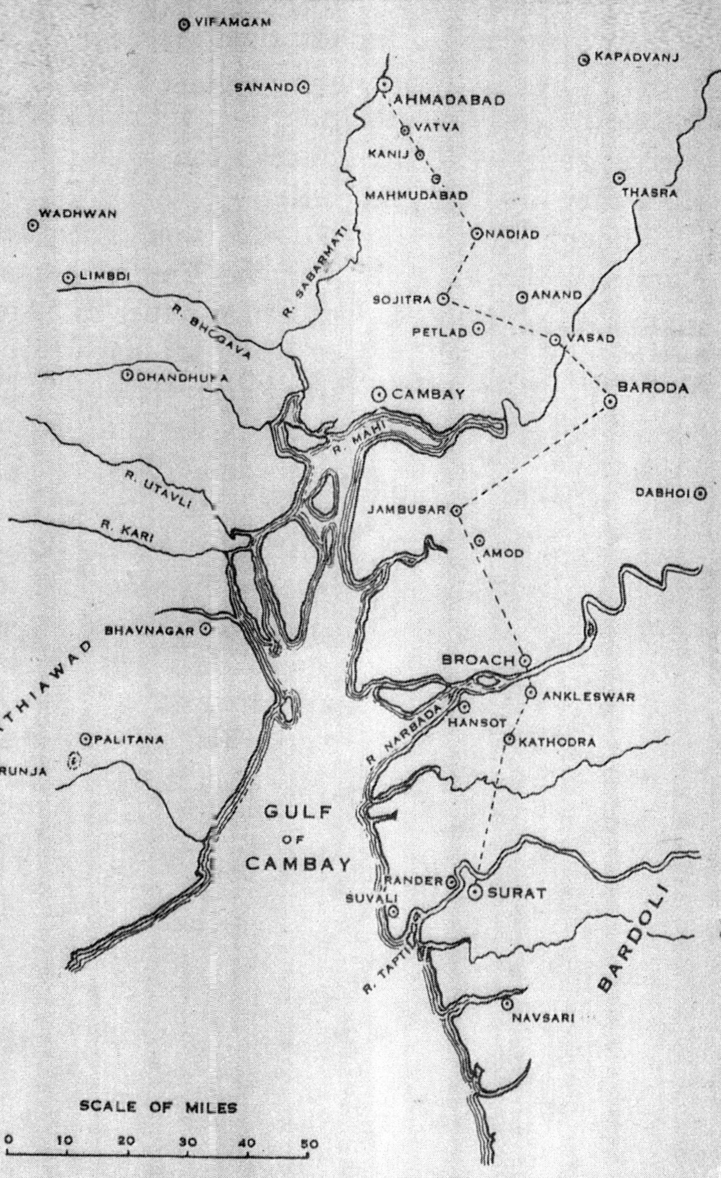

MAP OF MANDELSLO'S TOUR THROUGH GUJARAT

CHAPTER II

MANDELSLO'S JOURNEY FROM SURAT TO AHMADABAD

(30 SEPTEMBER TO 12 OCTOBER 1638)

Caravan sent by the English from Surat

THE *kafila*, or caravan, which Mandelslo joined at Surat on the last day of September 1638, was sent by the English President to Ahmadabad, and consisted of thirty wagons laden with quicksilver, spices and a considerable sum of money. The President had appointed four English merchants, a number of Banyas, twelve English armed soldiers and as many Indians, for conducting the same in safety. The young German traveller was thus assured that he could undertake the journey without any danger from the Rajputs who frequented the country and lived as robbers. These are described by Mandelslo's English translator as 'Tories or highwaymen'[1] who had their haunts in the mountains of Champaner and who often dared to insult the might of the Great Mogul from their fortified

[1] The sentence in Davies's translation of Mandelslo is as follows: 'These *Rasboutes* are a sort of Highwaymen, or Tories, who keep in the mountains between Brodra (Baroda) and Broitschia (Broach).'

'Tory' is the anglicized spelling of an Irish word which means either a pursuer, or a pursued or persecuted person. In the seventeenth century the term was applied to designate one of the dispossessed Irish who became outlaws and subsisted by plundering and killing the English settlers and soldiers. The word was then extended to mean robbers or bandits of other

retreats in the hills. The President himself and several of the factors accompanied their noble guest to a distance of a league (or about three miles) from the city, where they took leave of him.

Mandelslo finds some good game near Ankleswar

The caravan proceeded from Surat to Broach, passing through Kathodra,[1] which is described as a ruined place seated upon a river of the same name. Near Ankleswar, a good bag was secured by Mandelslo consisting of more than thirty wild duck and other waterfowl. The party also killed a roebuck and met with so many deer and wild pigs that there was no difficulty in providing themselves with good meals on the journey, the game being dressed by the cooks who accompanied them. Crossing the Narmada, they entered the city of Broach where the English agent or secretary invited them to dinner.

Broach described

Broach is described as a city standing upon a pretty high mountain, surrounded by walls of free-stone, 'and so well built that it may be numbered amongst the strongest places of all the Indies'. It had two large gates on the land side and two small ones towards the river, through which a great quantity of timber came into the town from distant parts. There was a Mogul

races, such as Border Moss-troopers, Scottish Highlanders and Rajput marauders or outlaws. The use of the word in this sense by J. Davies in 1662 in his translation of Mandelslo is quoted in the *Oxford English Dictionary*, vol. X, part 1, p. 171. Under Charles II the word 'Tory' came first to be applied as a nickname to the royalist opponents of the Exclusion Bill (1681).

[1] Kathodra is a small place in the Broach district, about nine miles south-west of Ankleswar.

guard or garrison posted in the fort, partly because of its military importance and also to collect the customs duty of two per cent upon all commodities that entered this port. The majority of the inhabitants were weavers who produced the famous *baftas* for which Broach was famous and which were 'finer than any made in the province of Gujarat'.[1] The lands round about the city were very fertile, yielding rice, wheat, barley and cotton in great abundance. In the mountains to the south-east of the town, which extended beyond Burhanpur, were found the agates from which were made the beautiful drinking cups, seals, handles for knives and daggers, and other rarities which were commonly manufactured in and sold at Cambay.[2] Eight leagues or about twenty-two miles further on from Broach, on the road leading to Cambay, stood the large village of Jambusar, famous for its great production of indigo, an industry which flourished at this place right up to the end of the eighteenth century.[3]

Arrival at Baroda: entertainment there

The English agent at Broach was also in charge of the factory at Baroda and, having some business at the latter town, he now accompanied the caravan. The journey was mostly done during the night, owing to the increasing heat, and the *kafila* arrived at

[1] Mandelslo, op. cit., p. 26. *Bafta* is derived from the Persian *baftan*, to weave.

[2] The agates and cornelians were found in the hills near Ratanpur in the present Rajpipla State.

[3] *Bombay Gazetteer*, vol. II, p. 564, 'Surat and Broach'. Jambusar is now a large town in the Broach district situated about five miles north of the Dhadhar river.

Baroda on 7 October. Here Mandelslo was entertained at a pleasant country-house where the English agent lived and which was originally a mausoleum. To add to his guest's enjoyment, the agent sent for some Hindu dancing girls who, says the traveller, 'were very desirous to see my clothes which I still wore after the German fashion, though the English and Dutch, who are settled in the Indies, go ordinarily according to the mode of the country and would have obliged me to put them off; but perceiving I was unwilling to do it, they seemed to be very much troubled and so went away.'[1] This reference is interesting, for it is not a generally accepted fact that the English and Dutch merchants settled in Gujarat adopted the ordinary dress of the country. Baroda was at this time fortified with good walls and bastions and had five gates, one of which was closed up as there was no high road leading from it. The inhabitants were mostly Hindus engaged in weaving, dyeing, etc.,

Lac industry in Gujarat

The flourishing village of Sankheda[2] situated twenty-two miles from Baroda, yielded annually 25,000 pounds of lac, a commodity which appears to have been produced in large quantities all over Gujarat at this period.[3]

[1] Mandelslo, op. cit., p. 27.

[2] Mandelslo describes the place as 'Sindickera, eight leagues from the city'. This is probably the present town of Sankheda in the subdivision of the same name in the Baroda State, separated from Bahadurpur by the river Or. There is an old fort at Sankheda.

[3] The name 'lac' is applied to the resinous incrustation formed on the bark of twigs of certain trees, by the action of the lac-insect, *Coccus lacca* (Watts, *Dictionary of the Economic Products of India*, vol. IV, p. 570).

Lac is described as being of a red-brown colour in its natural state. But when well dried and beaten to powder, the people could give it any colour they liked —black, red, green, yellow, etc. Besides being used extensively as sealing-wax, it was also employed for adorning and beautifying household furniture, such as chests, cabinets, tables, bedsteads, etc., giving to the articles such lustre as no one at the time could ever imitate in Europe, especially upon a black ground.[1]

The Mogul garrison at Vasad demands a toll

After leaving Baroda, Mandelslo proceeded with the caravan and reached the fort of Vasad[2] which he describes as an old castle, partly ruined, built upon a mountain. Here was stationed a Mogul garrison of a hundred horse, with permission to levy an impost of a rupee and a half, or about four shillings, on every waggon that passed by. But the English who led the caravan had obtained a passport from the Mogul officers by virtue of which they had been exempted from this levy. When the garrison stopped some of their carts in order to compel payment, the armed convoy opposed it and forced a passage through. Crossing the Mahi, the caravan encamped in a village on the opposite side of the river and made a barricade with the help of the carts to secure itself against a sudden attack. The same night, before the English had finished their supper, the leader of the Vasad

[1] Mandelslo, op. cit., p. 27.

[2] Vasad is a small place in the Kaira district on the main railway line from Bombay, twelve miles to the north of Baroda. It is situated on the Mahi which can be forded at this place. There are now no signs of any old castle or fortification.

garrison arrived with some thirty soldiers armed with pikes, swords, bucklers and guns, and desired an interview. He was permitted to come in accompanied by only three others and in reply to his demands was informed that the Mogul pass freed them from the duty, but that the English would make a free present of five or six rupees to show their goodwill. This offer was not accepted and the 'receiver' went away with the intention of returning the next morning.

Meanwhile a Dutch merchant, who was conducting a caravan of one hundred and seventy waggons, guarded by fifty Indian soldiers, arrived at the village and informed the English party that the soldiers belonging to the garrison had felled a great tree and had placed it across the road with the object of preventing their passage onward. It appeared that a stiff conflict would follow and there was actually some firing on both sides. Finding, however, that their opponents were at an advantage, those of the castle at last decided to come to a compromise and, making the Dutch merchant their intermediary, they represented to the English that they received no other pay than what they received from the tax on the merchandise passing that way and that, if they did not force merchants to pay this duty, there would be no means of subsistence left to them. They also declared their willingness to accept half the amount of the duty, but finding that this would not be forthcoming, they at last consented to take what had been originally offered, namely six rupees. The English were also very pleased with this amicable settlement as the numbers against them had increased to one hundred and, what was worse, the Indian sepoys whom they had engaged in the caravan refused to take up arms against the King's soldiers as unlawful and declared that their duty was to defend the caravan only against robbers who might attack it on the way. The incident, though of no historical importance, is nevertheless of great interest as it throws some interesting side-light on the conditions of travel in the Mogul Empire in the early part of the seventeenth century.

From Sojitra to Ahmadabad

The caravan continued its progress northwards and passing by the village of Sojitra[1] arrived at Nadiad, a centre for the production of both cottons and indigo. The next stage was Mahmudabad on the Vatrak river where the Banya population made a large quantity of cotton thread. Proceeding thence through Kanij, Vatva and Isanpur, at which last place there was a very fine caravanserai, it at last reached Ahmadabad, 'the metropolis of all Guzuratta,' on 12 October 1638. The journey of about one hundred and fifty miles from Surat had been accomplished within a period of twelve days.

English agent at the capital welcomes Mandelslo

Mandelslo proceeded a little in advance of the *kafila* and reached a garden, about a mile and a half outside the capital, which was probably the Kankaria Tank and sent word to the English agent at Ahmad-

[1] Sojitra is a town in the Petlad sub-division of the Baroda State.

abad of his arrival. The agent's name was Benjamin Roberts[1] and, on the information reaching him, he came up with his coach to receive his guest. It was a splendid equipage, gilt all over, covered with several pieces of rich Persian tapestry and drawn by two white oxen 'which expressed as much metal as we could have expected from the best horses in Germany.[2] By the side of the coach was led a very stately Persian horse, its harness being covered with plates of silver. After partaking of a collation of the little sack and English beer that was left with Mandelslo, Roberts took him in the coach and brought him into the city.

[1] Benjamin Robinson, not 'Roberts' as Mandelslo mentions, was chief of the English factory at Ahmadabad for several years.—*English Factories* (1637–41) edited by Wm. Foster, pp. 91, 225, 274.

[2] Mandelslo, op. cit., p. 29. The fine breed of Gujarat oxen was for centuries noted for its white colour, size and handsome appearance. Abul Fazl says that the Gujarat cattle were considered to be the finest in India and that a yoke of them was sometimes worth 100 mohurs. The best Gujarat oxen exceeded even swift horses in speed, for they could travel 120 miles in 24 hours. Akbar once bought a pair of cows for two lakhs of *dams* or 5,000 rupees.—Blochmann, *Ain-i-Akbari*, vol. I, p. 149.

CHAPTER III

MANDELSLO AT AHMADABAD

(OCTOBER 1638)

Mandelslo at the English factory in Ahmadabad

THE English factory, or lodge, at Ahmadabad was in the heart of the city, well-built, with many fine apartments and spacious courts for the storing of merchandise. 'Master' Roberts first brought his guest into his own chamber which overlooked a little flower garden with a fountain in it. The floor of this room was covered with tapestry and the pillars set out with silk stuffs of diverse colours, and above hung a large white tassel, as was customary in the houses of the great ones of the country. A spacious room was assigned to Mandelslo for his lodging. Supper was served in a great hall and, when it was over, the Dutch deputy in the city called with some of his merchants to see the visitor. After they had left, the whole company conducted the guest to his chamber, where Roberts kept him company till midnight. The warmth of the welcome could not be considered complete until six women dancers, the handsomest that could be found in the city, were sent for to entertain the guest. 'They admired my clothes,' writes Mandelslo, 'but, above all, that lock of my hair that hung down over my shoulders; and could hardly be induced to believe I was what I really am.'[1]

After resting for two days, the English agent took his guest in a coach to show to him some of the sights of Ahmadabad, at that time one of the proudest capitals of the Mogul Empire. They first came to the great market place which was called the Maidan Shah, or the royal square and which extended in front of the main gate of the Bhadra citadel. The account left of this park by Mandelslo deserves to be quoted to show how the present condition of the area contrasts with the lovely surroundings of three centuries ago:

Maidan Shah or royal square

'The Maidan Shah, or the king's market, is at least 1,600 feet long and half as many broad and beset all about with rows of Palm-trees and Date-trees, intermixed with Citron-trees and Orange-trees, whereof there are very many in the several streets: which is not only very pleasant to the sight, by the delightful prospect it affords, but also makes the walking among them more convenient by reason of the coolness. Besides this Maidan, there are in the city four Bazaars, or public places, where are sold all kinds of merchandise.'[2]

[1] Mandelslo, op. cit., p. 29. See Mandelslo's picture (*Frontispiece*) with the long locks so familiar to the Stuart period.

[2] Mandelslo, op. cit., pp. 29, 30. Compare with this Thevenot's account of the Maidan of Ahmadabad as seen in 1666, about thirty years after Mandelslo's visit: 'Going from their (Dutch) Lodgings, one enters by these high Arches (Three Gates) into the *Maidan-Shah*, which signifies the king's square. It is a long square having four hundred paces in breadth, and seven hundred in length, with trees planted on all sides. The Gate of the Castle is on the west side, opposite to the three Arches and the Gate of

The Bhadra castle was next visited and it is described as one of the most considerable in the whole kingdom. Inside the enclosure was the royal palace built of brick. Above its gate was a stage or curtain in which sat the musicians with their violins, oboes and bagpipes, which played four times a day, in the morning, at noon, in the evening and at midnight, as was the custom in Persia and all other countries under Moslem rule. All the apartments of the palace were sumptuous, being gilt and adorned with painting, 'but more to their satisfaction who are pleased with diversity of colours, than theirs who look for invention and stand upon the exactness of proportions.' After the inspection of the castle, they proceeded outside the town to see the imposing city walls which had twelve gates and were surrounded by a ditch sixteen fathoms broad. This was, however, in ruins in many places and without water.

The Bhadra castle and the royal palace within it

The next monument visited was the great Jain temple built only a few years before by Shantidas Jhaveri,[1] one of the wealthiest men of Gujarat in his day and high in favour both with Shah Jahan and after him

Shantidas' Jain temple at Saraspur

the Quervasaray on the south. On the same side are six or seven pieces of cannon mounted and on the other some more gates which are at the head of pretty fair streets. In this Maidan there are several little square buildings about three fathom high, which are Tribunals for the Kotwal who is the criminal judge. In the middle of the place there is a very high Tree, purposely planted for the exercise of those who learn to shoot with the bow and who with their arrows strive to hit a ball which for that end is placed on the top of the Tree.'—M. de Thevenot, *Travels into the Indies*, translated by Lovell, London (1687) p. 9.

[1] See Appendix I.

with Aurangzeb. The temple was situated outside the city to the east beyond the suburb of Saraspur; but even its ruins have now practically disappeared, the whole area being occupied by miserable dwellings peopled by factory hands. In 1638, however, when Mandelslo visited the place, this temple which he calls 'the principal mosque of the Banyas' was in all its pristine splendour and 'without dispute one of the noblest structures that could be seen'. 'It was then new,' he adds, 'for the Founder, who was a rich Banya merchant, named Shantidas, was living in my time."[1]

The great temple described

As Mandelslo's description is the earliest account we have of this famous monument, which was desecrated only seven years after his visit by the orders of Aurangzeb, then viceroy of Gujarat (1645),[2] we shall reproduce it at some length. It stood in the middle of a great court which was enclosed by a high wall of freestone. All about this wall on the inner side was a gallery,

[1] Mandelslo, op. cit., p. 30.

[2] The French traveller, M. de Thevenot, who visited the capital of Gujarat in 1666, says: 'Ahmadabad being inhabited also by a great number of Heathens, there are *Pagods* or Idol-Temples in it. That which was called the Pagod of Shantidas was the chief, before Aurangzeb converted it into a mosque. When he performed that ceremony, he caused a cow to be killed in the place, knowing very well that, after such an action, the Gentiles according to their Law, could worship no more therein. . . . The inside roof of the mosque is pretty enough, and the walls are full of the figures of men and beasts; but Aurangzeb, who hath always made a show of an affected devotion, which at length raised him to the Throne, caused the noses of all these figures, which added a great deal of magnificence to that Mosque, to be beat off.' —Thevenot, *Travels into the Indies*, London (1687) p. 10.

similar to the cloisters of the monasteries in Europe, with a large number of cells, in each of which was placed a statue in white or black marble. These figures no doubt represented the Jain Tirthankars, but Mandelslo may be forgiven when he speaks of each of them as 'representing a woman naked, sitting, and having her legs lying cross under her, according to the mode of the country'.[1] Some of the cells had three statues in them, namely, a large one between two smaller ones.[2] At the entrance to the temple stood two elephants of black marble in life-size and on one of them was seated an effigy of the builder. The walls of the temple were adorned with figures of men and animals. At the further end of the building were the shrines consisting of three chapels divided from each other by wooden rails. In these were placed marble statues of the Tirthankars with a lighted lamp before that which stood in the central shrine. One of the priests attending the temple was busy receiving from the votaries flowers which were placed round the images, as also oil for the lamps that hung before the rails, and wheat and salt as a sacrifice. The priest had covered his mouth and nose with a piece of linen cloth so that the impurity of his breath should not profane the images.

[1] Mandelslo, op. cit., p. 30.

[2] According to Jain iconography, the images of the Tirthankars are placed on highly sculptured thrones and surrounded by other smaller attendant figures. At the right of the Jina is a male figure representing the Yaksha attendant or servant of that particular Jina; at the left end of the throne is the corresponding female, or Yakshini, Yakshi or Sasanadevi; whilst in a panel in the middle there is often another devi.—Buhler and Burgess, *The Indian Sect of the Jainas*, pp. 62–63.

Mandelslo next gives us a description of Ahmadabad and an account of the principal commodities to be found there. It was a great and populous city, seven leagues, or about twenty miles, in compass including the suburbs and the adjacent villages. The streets were very broad, and the public and private buildings magnificent, especially the mosques and the residence of the provincial governor. A guard was kept in the city day and night and it had a considerable garrison. But Ahmadabad was unsurpassed at the time as a commercial emporium. 'There is not,' says Mandelslo, 'in a manner any nation, nor any merchandise in all Asia, which may not be had at Ahmadabad, where particularly there are made abundance of silks and cotton stuffs. . . . They also make there great quantities of gold and silver brocades, but they put too much thin lace into them, so that in goodness and substance they come not near those of Persia, though some of them amount in the country to eighteen crowns the piece.'[1]

Ahmadabad, a great commercial emporium

This testimony to the excellence of the silk manufactures of Ahmadabad is confirmed by the more elaborate references to the same by the French traveller, Tavernier, a generation later.[2] At the time when Mandelslo was there, a new kind of cloth was just beginning to be manufactured. It was a mixture of silk and cotton interwoven with flowers of gold,

Silk manufactures of the city

[1] Mandelslo, op. cit., p. 31.

[2] Tavernier, *Travels in India*, translated by Ball, vol. II, p. 3.

which was very highly esteemed and sold at five crowns per ell.[1] But the inhabitants were forbidden to wear it because the emperor had reserved the same for his own special use. It was, however, permissible for foreigners to buy it on condition that it was to be transported out of the Mogul empire. The other varieties of silks produced at Ahmadabad at this time were satins, velvets of all sorts of colours, taffetas and carpets on grounds of gold, silk or cotton.[2]

Other commodities exchanged at Ahmadabad

Among the other articles of commerce, besides silk and cotton cloths, to be commonly obtained in this city were sugar, whether as candy or in powder, cummin, honey, lac, opium, borax, ginger, myrabolams, saltpetre, sal ammoniac and indigo. Besides these, musk and ambergris[3] were also available in this capital, though they were not produced in Gujarat, but obtained from other parts. Ambergris was sold at forty *mahmudis*[4] or eight crowns per ounce and it came from Pegu and Bengal or from Mozambique and Cape Verd. Mandelslo makes special reference

[1] An ell is a cloth measure equal to one and a quarter yards.

[2] Mandelslo, op. cit., p. 31.

[3] Ambergris (grey amber) is a substance of the consistence of wax found floating in the Indian Ocean and other parts of the tropics, and also as a morbid secretion in the intestines of the sperm whale which is believed to be in all cases its true origin. It is highly valued in perfumery.

[4] The mahmudi was a silver coin, first minted in the reign of Sultan Mahmud I Begada (1458–1511), which was current in Gujarat for several centuries. The weight and value underwent frequent changes, but it may roughly be placed at equivalent to about half a rupee. For a full account of the history of this coin see *Ep. Ind.*, vol. IV, No. 42.

to the facility with which bills of exchange could be secured at Ahmadabad by merchants, the Banya shroffs having their correspondents in all parts of Asia, as also at Constantinople in Europe. This convenience was of the greatest advantage to traders in view of the terror of the Rajputs and others who infested the highways and made travelling very unsafe, in spite of all the expense undertaken by the Mogul power to maintain a considerable number of soldiers particularly for the safety of travellers. We are told that merchants had to pay no duties or customs at Ahmadabad on the export or import of goods, though it was usual to pay the *kotwal* fifteen pence per waggon by way of a present. Foreigners had freedom to trade in all sorts of commodities except those which were prohibited, such as gunpowder, lead and saltpetre, which articles were not allowed to be exported without the governor's permission. This was, however, not difficult to obtain for a consideration.

According to Mandelslo's information, the *suba* of Gujarat or Ahmadabad comprised within its jurisdiction twenty-five great towns and three thousand villages and its revenue amounted to more than six million crowns or one crore and twenty lakhs of rupees. From this amount the governor maintained twelve thousand horse whom he was obliged to keep for the royal service.

The Suba of Gujarat and its revenues

During his stay at Ahmadabad, which lasted

for nine or ten days, Mandelslo visited, among other sites, the village of Sarkhej, though his account of the saint's tomb there is far from accurate. His statement that the best indigo in the country was made here is, however, perfectly true.

Garden-like appearance of the capital and its suburbs

He also saw the Shahi Bag Gardens in the suburb of Begumpur and the famous Kankaria Tank. His reference to the garden-like appearance of Ahmadabad and its approaches is of interest and deserves to be quoted if only to contrast it with the present grimy surroundings of the city and its smoking chimneys:

'There are so many other gardens about Ahmadabat, and the whole city is so full of trees, that a man may say it makes all but one garden; for, as he comes to the city, he sees such abundance of them that he may well think he is going into a forest. Among other things I took particular notice of the Highway which they call Baschaban,[1] and leads to a village six leagues distant from the city. It is so straight that it should seem they took a great pleasure in planting the trees about it, whereof there is a double row on both sides upon a straight line. But this road comes nothing near that which goes from Agra to Barampour (Burhanpur) which

[1] This is probably the road leading to the Bagh-i-Shaban to the east of the city. During the reign of Sultan Qutb-ud-din of Gujarat (1451–8) his vizier, Malik Shaban, laid out this famous garden near the village of Rakhyal, about two miles east of Ahmadabad. The garden was surrounded by a wall and included a park, a mosque, a step-well and other buildings.—Nawab Ali and Seddon, *Suppt. to the Mirat-i-Ahmadi*, pp. 19, 20.

makes but one continued ally for a hundred and fifty German leagues together.'[1]

The apes a feature of the city

The large apes which are to-day so striking a feature of the city and suburbs of Ahmadabad and whose presence attracts the notice of every modern visitor to the capital, receive special mention on the part of Mandelslo when he is writing of the trees and gardens about the capital. Some of these apes were as large as greyhounds and strong enough to attack a man and they multiplied in great numbers owing to the strong objection of the Hindus to their being killed. This was due to their belief in metempsychosis, according to which 'the merriest and best humoured souls' among men returned into the bodies of apes after death. These monkeys were a source of special trouble to the vendors of fruit and preserves in the city and the German visitor counted one day a hundred and fifty of them at the English factory house at Ahmadabad. They played among themselves and indulged in a great many antics as if they were specially sent there for his diversion.

[1] Mandelslo, op. cit., p. 33.

FAÇADE OF AZAM KHAN'S SERAI AT AHMADABAD
Built 1637

CHAPTER IV

MANDELSLO'S VISITS TO AZAM KHAN, THE MOGUL GOVERNOR AT AHMADABAD

PERHAPS the most interesting portion of Mandelslo's account of his stay at Ahmadabad is that in which he refers to the governor of the province and his interviews with that potentate. This was the famous Azam Khan[1] whose long tenure of office in Gujarat is well known to students of history. He was about sixty years of age at this time, and our traveller was credibly informed that he was worth in money and household stuffs ten crores of rupees or fifty million crowns. Only a few months before this visit, his daughter, 'one of the greatest beauties in the coun-

Azam Khan, Governor of Gujarat: his wealth and establishment

[1] Mandelslo gives his name as Arab-chan (Khan) which is evidently a mistake. Azam Khan ruled Gujarat as governor for the unusually long period of seven years (1636–42) and restored peace and order in the province by subduing the lawless tribes of the Kolis near Viramgam and the Kathis near Dhandhuka. At Ranpur he erected an imposing castle, which still remains, to serve as a military outpost on the borders of Gujarat and Kathiawar. At Ahmadabad his memory has been perpetuated by the handsome caravanserai which he built in 1637 in the south-east corner of the Bhadra, a building which has for many years past been used as the head post-office of the city. The fort at the village of Kali, some miles to the north of Ahmadabad, was also probably constructed by Azam Khan. In spite of the success of his military expeditions, Azam Khan's administration of the province appears to have been ruthlessly oppressive, and when this condition of affairs was brought to the notice of Shah Jahan, the emperor ordered his recall in 1642.

try', had been married to Prince Shuja, the second son of the Emperor Shah Jahan. When this lady proceeded to the court for her wedding, her father had her attended by 20 elephants, 1,000 horse and 6,000 waggons laden with the richest and rarest stuffs in the province. Azam Khan's establishment consisted of 500 persons, of whom 400 were his slaves, who were maintained in his house and transacted his affairs. His domestic expenditure, for he entertained lavishly, amounted to about 5,000 crowns or 10,000 rupees a month, not including in this amount the money spent on the stables where he kept 500 horses and 50 elephants. The leading members of his retinue were magnificently clad, though he himself went in very plain cotton clothes. But when he appeared publicly in the city or made a journey into the country, he proceeded in great state, seated in a howdah upon an elephant which was caparisoned with the richest tapestry. On these occasions he was attended by a bodyguard of 200 soldiers and several standards and banners were carried before him, and many fine Persian horses accompanied him.[1]

On 18 October 1638, Mandelslo proceeded, along with the English chief, on a visit to the governor, whom they found sitting in a pavilion which overlooked his garden. After they were seated, Azam Khan asked of the English merchant the details about his companion. He replied that Mandelslo was a gentleman from Germany who had

[1] Mandelslo, op. cit., pp. 35, 36.

left his home with the desire of seeing foreign countries; that after proceeding to Persia with an embassy sent thither by his sovereign, he had decided to see the Indies, 'as being the noblest country in the world,' and having arrived at Ahmadabad he had made bold to aspire to the honour of waiting upon the governor. After asking whether he had, during his stay in Persia, learnt anything of the language of that country and being informed that he had made some attempt to study Turkish which was commonly spoken in the Shah's court, the governor wanted to know his age and how long it was since he had left Germany. Mandelslo made reply that he was twenty-four years old and had been on his travels for three years. The governor showed some surprise that his friends and relatives had allowed him to travel so young and inquired whether he had changed his dress on his journeys. Being informed in the negative, he declared that it was extremely fortunate that the young German should have travelled in that 'equipage' through so many countries without meeting with some unhappy incidents and added that the Dutch and the English residents in the province clad themselves according to the fashion of the country to prevent any such misfortune.

After about an hour's conversation, the visitors rose to take leave of the governor, but the latter requested them to stay and dine with him, an honour which was readily accepted. The dinner was a sumptuous affair served

Dinner at the governor's palace

up and prepared in the Persian manner. The meat was put in small dishes of porcelain upon rice of various colours in the same way as Mandelslo had seen done in the court of the Shah of Persia at Ispahan. After they had dined they took leave of Azam Khan who told Mandelslo at parting that he expected to see him again.

Second interview with Azam Khan: he transacts state business

In response to the desire thus expressed, both the English merchant and his guest paid a second visit to the governor two days later, on 20 October. On this occasion, however, Mandelslo had dressed according to the mode of the country, because he proposed the next day to travel to Cambay, which he thought it inexpedient to do without changing his costume. Azam Khan was clad in a white vestment over which there was another longer robe of brocade, the ground of it carnation lined with white satin and above a collar of sables of which the skins were sewn together so that the tails hung down over the back. The governor was attended on this occasion by a number of nobles and, as soon as he saw the European visitors, he bade them take their seats near them. Mandelslo soon realized from his remarks that he was pleased at the change in his dress. Though the governor was on this occasion engaged in disposing of state affairs, writing and despatching orders, he was not prevented from smoking tobacco, a servant holding the pipe to his mouth with one hand and setting fire to it with the other. The governor next left the apartment for a while to go out and review several companies of horse and foot which had been drawn up in the court. Being a seasoned and experienced commander, as our knowledge of his long governorship in Gujarat has made abundantly evident, he inspected their arms personally and made the troopers shoot at a mark in order to judge of their proficiency. The pay of such who did well at this exercise was augmented at the cost of the others who had done badly. Finding him thus occupied, Mandelslo and his guest wished to take their leave and in the interval had some fruit offered to them, the best part of which they forwarded to their house with his consent.

The Governor of Ahmadabad, a Persian born

Returning from the inspection, the governor called for a little golden cabinet set with precious stones. It had two small drawers, from one of which he took out some opium and out of the other *bhang*, a drug or powder made of the leaves and seed of the hemp plant. Having taken a small spoonful of each for himself, he sent round the cabinet to Mandelslo, saying that during his stay in Ispahan he must have learnt the use of this drug. Both the visitors helped themselves to a little of it, though neither had tasted the narcotic before, nor had much liking for the same. After this an animated conversation followed. Replying to an inquiry where he had learnt the Turkish language and whether he had ever visited Constantinople, Mandelslo said that he had not been to the Turkish capital, but had devoted his spare time in the province of Shirwan in Persia and at Ispahan in acquiring that tongue, the use of which was as common in Persia as that of the country. Azam Khan told his guest that Shirwan was his native country and he became naturally more friendly and talkative after this.

He dislikes Shah Safi of Persia

The conversation next turned on the character of Shah Safi of Persia,[1] for Mandelslo was able to say that he had come into close contact with that sovereign, had dined at his table and gone out hunting in his company. The governor was evidently no admirer of Shah Safi, for he wished to know whether that king still continued to be a tyrant, having begun his reign with the most bloody acts which had caused the death of a very large number of persons of all ranks. He declared that cruelty was hereditary in the Shah's family, having descended to him from his grandfather, Shah Abbas the Great.[2] Also that the famous Ali Mardan Khan, the Governor of Qandahar, had that very year transferred his allegiance to the great Mogul and delivered up to the latter this famous

[1] Shah Safi of Persia (1629–42) was the grandson and successor of Shah Abbas the Great, and his reign of thirteen years was one long chapter of executions. 'He murdered the princes of the royal blood and even some of the princesses and, not content with thus securing his power, deliberately put to death all his grandfather's most trusted councillors and generals.'—P. M. Sykes, *History of Persia*, vol. II, p. 297.

[2] Shah Abbas the Great, of the Safavi dynasty, ruled from 1587 to 1629, and takes rank with Charles V, Elizabeth and Akbar among the great rulers of the sixteenth century. The fame of his great achievements has been sullied by his ordering the murder or mutilation of three out of his four sons.

frontier stronghold, for no other reason but that he thought his life was in danger.

The governor contrasts the Persian and Mogul sovereigns

After these comments on the character and rule of Shah Safi of Persia, Azam Khan proceeded to some comparison between that ruler and his master, the great Mogul, who was at this time the Emperor Shah Jahan. What followed may better be given in Mandelslo's own language:

'He (the governor) was content to believe that Shah Safi was an understanding person, but that even as to that there was no more comparison between him and the Mogul than there was between the poverty of the one and the vast wealth of the other, the Prince his master being able to maintain a war against three kings of Persia. I was loath to enter into any contestation upon so ticklish a subject and therefore only told him that it was indeed true that there was not any comparison between the gold and the silver; the wealth of Persia and what I had already seen of the Mogul's kingdom; but that it must be withal confessed that Persia had one thing which could not be had elsewhere and was in effect inestimable, which was the great number of Kazilbashis[1] with whose assistance the King of Persia might attempt the conquest of all Asia: which I said purposely, knowing the

[1] Kazilbash, or 'Red Head,' was the name given to seven Turkish tribes known for their valour. These tribesmen were so called because they wore a scarlet head-piece. They professed the Shiah faith and it was with their help that the founder of the great Safavi dynasty had established his power in Persia.—Sykes, *Persia*, vol. II, p. 242 and *n*.

governor was a Kazilbash and that he could take no offence at such a discourse. Accordingly, he discovered his satisfaction thereat, not only in saying that he must grant it to be true, but also when turning to one of the lords, who was a Persian, as well as himself, he said to him, "I believe this young gentleman hath courage when he speaks so well of those that have." '[1]

The character of the Governor of Ahmadabad

The discourse having ended, dinner was served. A number of large vessels were brought in and the carver who sat in their midst filled the little dishes with a huge spoon, which were then served up to the party. The Khan himself, to assure the guests of his pleasure at their company, added with his own hand something to their plates. The room in which the refreshment was given was full of military officers, some of whom stood on guard with half-pikes in their hands, while others sat about a tank or reservoir which was in the room. After dinner was over, the visitors took their leave. Mandelslo describes the governor as 'a judicious, understanding man, but hasty and so rigorous that his government inclined somewhat to cruelty'. To illustrate this, he relates the following incident of the dancing girls who were executed in his palace for refusal to obey his summons:

'It happened one day that the two principal directors of the English and Dutch trade there being invited by him to dinner, . . . jesting with

[1] Mandelslo, op. cit., pp. 37, 38.

the English merchant put him into so good a humour that he would needs devote the remainder of the day to sport and divertisement and thereupon sent for twenty women-dancers who, as soon as they were come into the room, fell a-singing and dancing, but with an activity and exact observation of the cadence much beyond that of our dancers upon the ropes. They had little hoops or circles, through which they leaped as nimbly as if they had been so many apes and made thousands of postures according to the several soundings of their music, which consisted of a timbrel, an oboe and several tabours. Having danced near two hours, the governor would needs send into the city for another band of dancers, but the servants brought word that they were sick and could not come. This excuse being not taken, he sent out the same servants with express order to bring those women away by force; but they returning the second time with the same excuse, he ordered they should be cudgelled. Upon that, they cast themselves at the governor's feet, and acknowledged that it was indeed true they were not sick, but that they absolutely denied to come, saying they knew well enough the governor would not pay them. He laughed at it, but immediately commanded out a party of his guard to bring them to him, and they were no sooner entered into the hall, ere he ordered their heads to be struck off. They begged their lives with horrid cries and lamentations; but he would be obeyed and caused the execution to

Execution of the dancing girls

be done in the room before all the company, not one of the lords then present daring to make the least intercession for those wretches, who were eight in number. The strangers were startled at the horror of the spectacle and inhumanity of the action which the governor taking notice of fell a-laughing and asked them what they were so much startled at? "Assure yourselves, gentlemen," said he, "that if I should not take this course, I should not be long governor of Ahmadabad. For should I connive once at their disobedience they would play the masters and drive me out of the city. 'Tis prudence in me to prevent their contempt of my authority by such examples of severity as these are."'[1]

[1] Mandelslo, op. cit., pp. 38, 39. There is no reason to discredit this circumstantial account, for Azam Khan had a reputation for severity even before he was appointed Governor of Gujarat in 1636. On the news of his appointment reaching Ahmadabad, the leading inhabitants of the city forwarded a petition to the Emperor Shah Jahan requesting him to continue Saif Khan as governor. Though the latter had sufficiently abused his powers, the people of Ahmadabad evidently feared worse usage under his successor.—*English Factories in India* (1634–6) edited by Foster, p. 259.

CHAPTER V

MANDELSLO AT CAMBAY

AFTER spending some nine days at Ahmadabad, Mandelslo started, on 21 October, for a short visit to Cambay. As robbers were known to infest the highway, a convoy of eight foot-soldiers, armed with pikes and bucklers, was engaged for the journey. The men served also as lackeys and were hired for the small sum of eight crowns or sixteen rupees for the journey. Proceeding by the village of Fateh Wadi to Sojitra, Mandelslo at last reached Cambay on the third day. Here he was met by a Banya broker in the service of the English and Dutch companies, who knew Portuguese, and brought him into the town. As the English agent in Cambay was away from the city, the broker arranged for Mandelslo's lodging with a Mohammedan merchant of the place.

Mandelslo's trip to Cambay

Cambay is described as a walled city with a dozen gates, very large houses, straight and broad roads and much greater in extent than Surat. The majority of the inhabitants were Hindus, who applied themselves to commerce, and carried on an extensive business with Achin, Div, Goa, Mecca and Persia. They exported to these places all sorts of silk and cotton stuffs and brought back in exchange gold

Description of the city and its gardens

and silver in the form of ducats, sequins and rials. After spending two hours looking after the sites in the city, Mandelslo was taken by the broker outside the walls, where he was shown some fifteen public gardens. Among these one near the seashore, which contained the mausoleum of the founder and was surrounded by a high wall, is specially selected for encomium. 'There is not,' says our traveller, 'any place in all those parts that hath so noble a prospect as this, not only towards the seaside, but also towards the land where a man hath the sight of the noblest champion country in the world. This is so pleasant a place that the Mogul (emperor), being one day at Cambay, would needs take up his lodging in the garden and caused the stones of the sepulchre to be taken away that his tent might be pitched there.'[1]

Mogul policy towards the Hindu custom of sati

Mandelslo was soon joined by two of the English merchants of the factory at Cambay who offered to take him the next morning to a place near the city where an Indian widow was to burn herself and become a *sati*. The woman's husband was a Rajput who had been killed near Lahore, upon news of which she declared her determination to put an end to her life. The Governor of Cambay had for a long time opposed her desire since it was the policy of the Mogul government and its officers to abolish by degrees this 'heathenish and barbarous custom.' He pretended that as the news of her husband's death had not been confirmed, he could not give his

[1] Mandelslo, op. cit., p. 40.

consent to the action which she contemplated and for which there might be cause to repent afterwards. His object was to see whether the lapse of time would abate her passion to follow her husband into the other world. At last, finding that she was becoming daily more and more insistent in her resolve, he permitted her to comply with the practices of her religion. Mandelslo here correctly describes the imperial attitude towards this ancient custom. No Hindu widow could, since Akbar's time, immolate herself without the formal sanction of the governor, but the latter could only advise and delay his decision; if the woman remained firm he was bound to grant the permission.[1]

Mandelslo describes the ceremony which he witnessed

The young woman, who had decided to sacrifice herself to show her love for her husband, was not more than twenty years of age. But she came up to the place prepared for the funeral pyre with so much self-control and cheerfulness so unusual

[1] The French traveller, M. de Thevenot, also refers to the policy of the Moslem governors to prevent the burning of Hindu women after their husbands' death: 'To conclude, the women are happy that the Mohammedans are become the masters in the Indies to deliver them from the tyranny of the Brahmins who always desire their death, because these ladies being never burnt without all their ornaments of gold and silver about them, and none but they having power to touch their ashes, they fail not to pick up all that is precious from amongst them. However, the great Mogul and other Mohammedan princes, having ordered their governors to employ all their care in suppressing that abuse, as much as lies in their power, it requires at present great solicitations and considerable presents for obtaining the permission of being burnt; so that the difficulty they meet with in this secures a great many women from the infamy they would incur in their caste if they were not forced to live by a Superior Power.'—Thevenot, *Travels into the Indies*, London (1687) p. 85.

in a person who is faced with inevitable death that Mandelso was much inclined to believe that she had dulled her senses with a dose of opium. The description which he gives of the melancholy scene, and of the procession accompanying the woman, is similar to the accounts given by other old travellers who witnessed such sacrifices in India. Having looked upon the pyre with a certain amount of disdain, the young widow took leave of her kindred and her friends and distributed among them her rings and bracelets and other ornaments. 'I was,' says the German traveller, 'something near her on horseback, with the two English merchants, and I think she perceived in my countenance that I pitied her, whence it came that she cast me one of her bracelets which I had the good hap to catch and still keep in remembrance of so extraordinary an action.'[1]

Visits Mirza Beg, a leading merchant, and receives presents

The same day, Mandelslo paid a visit to one of the leading merchants of Cambay, named Mirza Beg, to whom he had brought letters of recommendation from the chief of the English factory at Ahmadabad. They had some general talk and exchange of compliments in the Turkish language. After Mandelslo had returned home and finished his meals, there came a man bearing some presents from Mirza Beg, namely twelve capons and pullets, a basket of eggs, a pannier of coco-nuts, a great bundle of sugar-canes and a very fine vessel

[1] Mandelslo, op. cit., p. 41.

made of agate. The next morning, as Mandelslo was departing for Ahmadabad, hoping to call on the merchant on the way to thank him for his presents, the latter himself turned up to wish him good-bye. The German requested him to accept a fine pocket-pistol made in London. The merchant replied that it was ungracious to receive presents from a stranger, but that it would be a greater act of incivility to refuse what had been so kindly proffered and that he would accept the gift which had been bestowed on him though he was little deserving of the same. Here Mandelslo in his diary enters some reflections which are as complimentary to the people of India as they are spontaneous and indicative of a discerning and noble disposition on the part of the writer:

'I give a particular account of this answer,' says he, 'that the reader may judge thereby whether those persons who are so well furnished with compliments of this nature should be looked on as barbarians; and no doubt but he will be much more surprised when I shall tell him that there is more civility to be found among the Indians than there is among those who pretend to the sole possession of it, but seldom accompany it with the sincerity which ever attends it in the Indies, where such as are friends are such without any finesse or reservation to those to whom they have promised friendship; as they are, on the other side, irreconcilable enemies to such as have injured them.'[1]

[1] Mandelslo, op. cit., p. 42.

The offer of the usual compliment of betel-nut and *pan* to Mirza Beg before he departed leads Mandelslo to a long dissertation on their universal use in India and their history and production. He adds some interesting details about the hold which these articles had obtained on such Europeans as were domiciled in India for any length of time. This was particularly the case with the Portuguese women at Goa, 'who are perpetually employed about this exercise, chewing this drug as cows and such other cattle chew the cud.'[1] He admits that the frequent use of this luxury discolours the teeth which turn a red colour, but adds that that is considered one of the beauties of the Indian women. The nobles of the country had these digestives carried about with them in boxes of lac or silver, and ate them as they went about the streets, or even when they had weighty business to transact.

Remarks on the use of betel and *pan* in India

Travelling the same way by which he had come, Mandelslo reached the village of Sojitra so late at night that the Jain shopkeepers, who did not burn candles for fear of some insects being thereby destroyed, would not open their shops to sell the traveller any forage for his beasts. The latter was thinking of breaking open one of the shops rather than allow his horses and oxen to starve, when one of the Banyas provided him with some forage which in these parts consisted of sugar and meal with the

The Jain shopkeepers of Sojitra

[1] Mandelslo, op. cit., p. 43.

FATEH WADI, OR THE GARDEN OF VICTORY, NEAR SARKHEJ ON THE SABARMATI, AHMADABAD

Built c. 1584

addition of a little butter at times. After another day's journey the party arrived at the famous garden of Fateh Wadi on the Sabarmati near Sarkhej.

Mandelslo visits the Jitbag or Fateh Wadi near Sarkhej

On his outward journey to Cambay, Mandelslo had reached the place at night. But on the present occasion he was able to have a good look at Fateh Wadi and its pleasure-houses which had been constructed at the end of the sixteenth century by Akbar's general, Abdurrahim Khan, the son of Bairam Khan, to commemorate his great victory in 1583–4 over the last of the Gujarat sultans.[1] Mandelslo's description of this garden is fuller than any given by the Persian historians or by other European travellers and deserves to be reproduced:

One of the loveliest gardens in all India

'This garden which, no doubt, is the most delightful of any in the Indies, is also the most considerable of any in the whole country, not only in respect of the victory which the Mogul gained in that place over the last king of Guzuratta, and which gave it the name of Zzietbag (Jitbag), that is to say, the *garden of victory*; but also in respect of its magnificent structures and the noble fruits which grow there in great abundance. It is seated in one of the most pleasant places in the world, upon the side of a great Pool, having on the side towards

[1] The picture in this chapter illustrates the Pleasure House built on the river at Fateh Wadi by Akbar's famous general. But for considerable private expenditure on repairs and conservation by Mr. Nariman R. Kothawala who holds this estate, the ruins of this imposing and historic structure would by this time have completely disappeared.

the water several Pavilions, and on that towards Ahmadabat a very high wall. The sumptuousness of the buildings speaks the great spirit of the Prince that founded it, as doth also the caravansarai adjoining thereto.

'There are in the garden many alleys of fruit-trees: as orange and citron-trees of all sorts; pomegranate-trees, date-trees, almond-trees, mulberry-trees, and trees which bear tamarinds, mangoes and cocos, besides many other not known to us; and there was such abundance of them, and they were planted so close that we could walk about the Garden in the shade, which was a great refreshing to us. The branches of all these trees were infinitely stored with apes, which added not a little to the divertisement and satisfaction of our walk. We stayed no longer in it than while our horses were baiting, in regard we were resolved to get that day to Amadabat, whither we came at night."[1]

Mandelslo proceeds to Agra and Lahore

Mandelslo did not, after his return from Cambay, stay for more than a day or two at Ahmadabad, having been informed that a caravan of two hundred merchants was ready to start for the Mogul capital at Agra. On 28 October, therefore, he left the city for the tour northwards to Hindustan, being recommended to the leader of the caravan by the English president at Surat. Having, after a long journey, reached Agra, Mandelslo proceeds to give a long account of the court and the government of the great Mogul

[1] Mandelslo, op. cit., p. 44.

and his wealth and revenues, a subject on which it is not necessary to enter in this book.[1] From Agra, after a short stay, the German proceeded to Lahore, where he entered one of the many public *hamams* and enjoyed the luxury of a Turkish bath. But his stay here was soon cut short by the arrival of letters from Agra to the effect that Methwold, the English President at Surat, intended very shortly to embark for England. Mandelslo, who desired to accompany him on the voyage to Europe, put himself in the company of several Indian merchants who were proceeding to Ahmadabad, and in due course arrived again in that city, some time in December 1638.

[1] Mandelslo, op. cit., pp. 45-57. This is a fairly long interpolation by de Wicquefort or by Olearius.

CHAPTER VI

MANDELSLO'S RETURN JOURNEY TO SURAT AND HIS LAST DAYS IN GUJARAT

AT Lahore, Mandelslo had received letters from President Methwold to say he was waiting only for the arrival of the *kafilas* from Agra and Ahmadabad, and would depart for England as soon as the goods which they brought with them reached Surat and were put on board ship. The President also informed him that he was shortly delivering over charge of his office and as there would be great entertainments and feasting on the occasion he would be glad of Mandelslo's presence. The latter, therefore, started from Ahmadabad for Surat as soon as the caravan from Agra had arrived and was accompanied by the director of the factory at Ahmadabad, who as well as his second were to be present at the ceremony when the President was to hand over charge.

Recalled by President Methwold

The return journey to the seaport of Surat was by the same route by which Mandelslo had come, but it was destined to be much more eventful. The caravan had left Mahmudabad, Vasad and Baroda, and was nearing Broach when it was attacked by a large band of Rajput highwaymen. A sharp conflict took

Eventful journey from Ahmadabad to Surat

place in which the robbers were ultimately forced to withdraw. The armed soldiers in the *kafila* took part in the fight, as also did Mandelslo and the English merchants with him. His account of the engagement deserves to be quoted:

Sharp skirmish with Rajput robbers near Broach

'Accordingly almost ere we could resolve how to make our party good against them, we saw coming out of all sides of the wood a great number of Rasboutes (Rajputs) armed with short pikes, bucklers, bows and arrows, but without any firearms. We had the time to charge those we had, which were four firelocks and three pair of pistols. The merchant and I got on horseback and bestowed the firelocks among those who were in the coach, with express order not to fire till they were sure to do execution. Our firearms were charged with square pieces of steel and the Rasboutes came on in so close a body that at the first firing we saw three fall. They shot certain arrows at us, wherewith they hurt an ox and two foot-soldiers. One was shot into the pommel of my saddle and the English merchant had another shot into his turbaut. The Dutch *kafila* hearing the noise commanded out ten soldiers; but ere they could come in to our relief we ran a great hazard of our lives. For I was set upon on all sides and was thrust twice with a pike into my buff-collar which certainly saved my life that day. There came two of the Rasboutes so near as to lay hold on my bridle, after they had killed two of my foot-soldiers, and were going to carry me away prisoner. But I dispatched one of them with a pistol shot, which I gave him in the shoulder, and the English merchant came in to my relief and behaved himself with as much gallantry as it was possible man could do. The ten foot-soldiers belonging to the Dutch *kafila* being come in and the *kafila* itself not much behind them, the Rasboutes got into the woods, leaving six men killed upon the place and carrying along with them many hurt. On our side we had two foot-soldiers killed and eight wounded, besides whom the English merchant had also received a slight wound.'[1]

Conditions of travel in Gujarat

We have given a fairly long extract of this engagement from Mandelslo's work as it helps to illustrate the general conditions of travel in Gujarat under Mogul rule in the first half of the seventeenth century. It is interesting, besides, for the light it throws on Mandelslo's personal bravery and that of his companion, but for whom and the soldiers under them, the caravan would undoubtedly have been mercilessly looted by the robbers. There were no further mishaps on the journey and passing through Broach and Ankleswar the party at last reached Surat on 26 December 1638.

Methwold formally delivers over charge

At Surat, Mandelslo found some fifty English merchants assembled at the factory house, many of whom had been summoned by the President from the subordinate factories in Gujarat and other parts to

[1] Mandelslo, op. cit., p. 59.

render an account of their administration as well as to be present at the change in the presidentship. Besides Methwold the President[1] and Fremlin his second, who was to succeed him in this office, the party included five 'consuls' from several factories in the Indies, three chaplains, two physicians and the rest merchants. At the formal ceremony of handing over charge in the presence of the assembled company, Methwold delivered an excellent address thanking those present for the many proofs he had received during his term of office of their fidelity and affection and for the honour and respect which they had rendered the East India Company in his person. He requested them to give the same allegiance to Fremlin, who had been his second, and to whom he was resigning his charge according to orders received. He concluded by exhorting them to behave in all matters in a manner that would conduce most to the reputation and advantage of the company. After this he handed over to his successor the letters patent by virtue of which he was to assume the new charge and made some complimentary remarks about him.[2]

When this official ceremony was over, Methwold and the whole assembly went to their garden outside the city where the President had arranged

[1] Methwold was chief of the English factory at Surat for seven years (1631–8) and stood head and shoulders above his immediate predecessors in ability and character. In 1636 President Methwold had been imprisoned by the Surat governor, Hakim Massih-uz-Zaman, for piracies at sea for which neither the chief nor his masters in England were in any way responsible.

[2] Mandelslo, op. cit., pp. 59, 60.

a magnificent entertainment for his guests, consisting of whatever was excellent and rare that could be procured in the country. Besides the refreshments, there was present a band of English music (violins), another of Muslim music and a third of Hindu, which last was accompanied by the inevitable women dancers for the further entertainment of the company. After the party had broken up, orders were issued that those ships which had been fully laden with cargo should make all necessary preparations for the return journey. Mandelslo and the others who were to go in them also made things ready for the long voyage to Europe.

He entertains the factors magnificently

The change of presidents in the English factory at Surat in the last days of the year 1638 coincided with a change in the Mogul governors of the city. Mandelslo gives the name of the new incumbent as Mirza Mahmud[1] and describes his state entry into the town on 28 December. The new President, Fremlin, went half a league or about a mile and a half out of the city to meet him and was accompanied by five of the most important factors who requested Mandelslo to go along with them. In front of the governor's procession was a company

Procession of Mir Musa's state entry into Surat

[1] Mandelslo is not correct. The name of the new ruler was Mir Musa (Muiz-ul-Mulk) who was appointed for the second time as governor of Surat and Cambay at the end of 1638 in succession to Hakim Massih-uz-Zaman whose rule at Surat had proved thoroughly cruel and oppressive. Mir Musa's second term of office lasted for three years and he was recalled in 1641.—*English Factories in India* (1637–41) edited by Foster, p. 279.

of infantry and a number of palankeens, and after these came an elephant on which sat a man carrying a banner of red taffeta. The elephant was followed by about a hundred foot-soldiers, behind whom were twenty others each of whom carried a little banner in his hand, 'much like those of our cornets,' in several colours. Then came the governor mounted upon a fine Persian horse and attended by several persons of quality and a great number of officers on horseback. At the tail end of the procession was carried the governor's palankeen, gilt all over. The people thronged the streets and received their new ruler with loud acclamations. After accompanying him to his palace, the new President returned to his own house.[1]

Mandelslo's last days in Gujarat

On 1 January 1639 Methwold, having made all arrangements for the voyage, went to take leave of the new governor who received him kindly and presented him with a vestment of brocade, the collar of which was made of 'two martin's skins with sables', and many other rare articles. Leaving the palace, Methwold and Mandelslo stepped into a shallop and proceeded by the river to the *Mary* which was lying in the roadstead. The new President and the chief officers in the English factory accompanied them to the ship where they all stayed three days 'entertaining and treating one another, and drowning in good wine the affliction which was to ensue upon

[1] At this place in the *Travels* we have a long interpolation on the province of Gujarat covering twenty-eight folio pages (pp. 60–88). It is entirely an addition by de Wicquefort, the French translator.

so long a separation '.[1] The long voyage to Europe began on the fifth day of the new year, the ship touching at Daman, Bassein and Goa on her way to the Cape.[2]

Value of his *Travels* in the history of Gujarat

Mandelslo's tour in Gujarat and his stay at Surat and Ahmadabad supply a unique picture of the condition of the province, the life of the people and the manners of the age, which it is impossible to secure from any of the formal histories of the time. For the historian of Gujarat his work has thus a value which the writings of the more famous travellers of the seventeenth century, such as Bernier, Tavernier and Manucci cannot possess.

[1] Mandelslo, op. cit., p. 89.

[2] The following is an extract from a long letter entitled 'President Fremlen and Council, aboard the *Mary* at the mouth of the Surat river, to the Company, January 4, 1639':

'Methwold has availed himself of the permission given in the letters received by the *Jonas* to resign his position, and now goes home in the *Mary*. . . . There is a young gentleman named John Albrecht Van Manslo (Mandelslo), who accompanied the Duke of Holstein's ambassador by the Caspian Sea to the King of Persia. When the ambassador returned, this gentleman, whether out of curiosity or discontent, made choice to come for India. And arriving here with the *Swan* about the end of April, he hath lived ever since amongst us, the civillest, modestest, and fairest behaved that we have ever known of his age and education. He declareth that it was his purpose to seek a passage by sea, which he hoped to have found at his first arrival. We made little difficulty to grant it him; but withal we declared ourselves to be servants, and therefore left him accountable to you for the diet and passage of himself and servant; whereunto he willingly submitted. He pretendeth to have some near relation to the Duke of Holstein, as having been sometimes his page, as he had been to Count Wallenstein, Duke of Friedland. You may please to approve of this our accommodation of him, since in truth we conceive he doth well deserve it.'—*English Factories in India* (1637-41) edited by Foster, p. 118.

CHAPTER VII

MANDELSLO'S VISIT TO GOA

THE *Mary*, with the English President and Mandelslo on board, set sail from Surat bar on 5 January 1639, and got the same night in sight of the town of Daman. The reference which our traveller makes to the siege of Daman,[1] which was invested by the Mogul army at this period, is of great interest as a proof of the credibility of his narrative:

The ship calls at Daman which is besieged by the Mughals

'The governor sent us a vessel of wine, about the bigness of a barrel, and some other refreshments, notwithstanding the siege which the King of Deccan, his neighbour, then maintained against the place, but with little good success, in regard the haven being not blocked up, the Indians could not prevent the sending in of relief into the city, even in the day-time.'[2]

[1] This was the great siege of Daman in 1638–9 during the reign of Shah Jahan. The city was invested from the land side by a Mogul army of 5,000 foot and as many horse under the command of a general who was acting under the orders of Prince Aurangzeb, then viceroy of the Deccan provinces, with his headquarters at Daulatabad. The siege lasted for many months for the garrison kept up a spirited defence, the sea being open to them for receiving supplies. At last a settlement was effected through the efforts of Mir Musa, the Governor of Surat, who was helped in the matter by President Fremlin of the English factory.—*English Factories in India* (1637–41) edited by Foster, pp. 123–4, 203, 214–6.

[2] Mandelslo, op. cit., p. 89. Here follows an interpolation by Olearius on the kingdom of the Deccan, etc., covering some eight pages of the text (pp. 89–97).

Two days later, the ship reached Bassein, then in the possession of the Portuguese, where it was welcomed with seven guns. Here, at the governor's desire, a frigate belonging to this nation was allowed to accompany the ship under the English colours in order to escape falling into the hands of the Dutch who were constantly moving up and down the coast. On 9 January the *Mary* passed by the islands of Bandra and Bombay, and on the 11th it entered the harbour of the great city of Goa.[1]

Passes by Bassein and arrives at Goa

As Methwold had some important financial affairs to settle at Goa,[2] he and his German com-

[1] This was Old Goa, the famous city founded by Albuquerque in 1510, near the site of the town conquered by him from the Bijapur State. By the end of the sixteenth century it had grown into one of the finest capitals in India with a large population, stately buildings and extensive commerce, and it was a current proverb to say: 'If you have seen Goa, you needn't go to Lisbon.' After the middle of the seventeenth century its decline began, first owing to the attacks of the Dutch whose fleets blockaded the harbour, and also because, its site becoming pestilential, the city began to be deserted. 'It is now literally a city of ruins, and is so hidden from view by the foliage of the jungle which has occupied it that the stranger approaches it unawares, and drives into the midst unconscious that he is traversing streets of ruined, empty dwellings, occupied by coco-nut and other tall trees instead of human beings. In the midst of all this ruin Goa remains a city of magnificent churches, four or five ranking as first class and in perfect preservation.'—*Murray's Handbook for Travellers in India* (1926) p. 492.

[2] President Methwold specially called at Goa on his homeward voyage to secure the payment of a large sum of money due to the Surat factory from the Portuguese authorities at Goa, a matter which had been long pending settlement. According to Mandelslo (p. 60) he was 'to receive fifty thousand rials, which the Portuguese were to pay in execution of the treaty of peace they had made with the English, to be employed in the Indies according as the President of Surat should dispose thereof.' See also *English Factories in India* (1637–41) edited by Foster, pp. 111, 203.

panion remained as guests in the capital of Portuguese India for ten days. A visit from the English President at Surat to the city of Goa was an event of special importance, and he was accordingly received with the highest honours. The Portuguese admiral, described as the 'General of the Galleons', who was then in the port with his fleet to operate against the Dutch squadron, welcomed the President with a volley from his largest guns, and soon after came up in person on board the *Mary* in a gilt gondola covered with scarlet cloth. After these formalities were over, the President left his ship and proceeded up the river to the city with his trumpets sounding before him. On arrival at Goa, his first visit was to the house of the *Fiador de la Fazenda* or the 'Overseer of the Exchequer',[1] it being with him chiefly that he was to negotiate the business which had occasioned his calling at Goa. This officer was sick in bed, but received his visitor with great civility, and as they had long been friends promised to give him all possible help. Methwold was then conducted in a palankeen to the residence arranged for him; and having asked for an audience with the viceroy[2] immediately

The President received with high honours

[1] The office of *Fiador da Fazenda* was the most important at Goa next to that of the viceroy. 'As there was no efficient audit of his accounts, and it was no crime for a Portuguese at this period to cheat the King of Spain, his embezzlements were on a vast scale.'—*Voyage of Pyrard de Laval*, translated by Gray and Bell, Hakluyt Society (1887) vol. II, p. 21 *n*.

[2] The viceroy's name was Dom Pedro da Silva de Menezes (1635-9). He died on 24 June 1639, some months after Mandelslo's visit.—Danvers, *Portuguese in India*, vol. II, p. 267.

proceeded to wait on the latter who lived in royal style at Goa.

Interview with the Viceroy of Goa

The viceroy's palace lay on the river side, and Methwold and his companions proceeded thither by boat. They were met by several *fidalgos* or gentlemen of the viceroy's retinue who conducted them into the hall where the audience was to be given and which was richly furnished and full of pictures of several princes of Europe.[1] The guards, who were clad in livery, presented arms and stood in two files in the antechamber through which the hall was to be entered.[2] The viceroy, who was dressed in black, rose from his chair at the President's coming in and did not sit down again till the other was seated. All the rest of the company stood before the viceroy except some of the gentlemen who conducted Mandelslo and others into one of the side rooms to entertain them. The President having discussed his business took leave of the viceroy, who brought him to the hall-

[1] These were life-size paintings of all the viceroys who had ruled in the Indies, and not portraits of European princes as Mandelslo writes. This interesting gallery of paintings is still preserved in the palace of the governors at Panjim or New Goa. There is little doubt that the coloured portraits of the viceroys in the Resenda MS at the British Museum are copies of these paintings.—*Pyrard de Laval*, op. cit., vol. II, p. 50 and *n*. Another large reception-hall in the viceroy's palace contained paintings of all the fleets and vessels which had gone from Portugal to the Indies, each bearing the name of the ship and of the captain and the number of guns it carried.—ibid., p. 50 and Tavernier, *Travels in India*, translated by Ball, London (1889) vol. I, p. 187.

[2] These guards formed a company of 100 men, all clad in blue livery. They were Portuguese, carried halberts, and kept close to the viceroy's person in the palace or wherever he went.—*Pyrard de Laval*, op. cit., vol. II, p. 51.

door and stood bare till the visitors were all gone. The gentlemen of his retinue accompanied the guests to their boat on the river, showing them on the way twelve fine horses, sumptuously covered and harnessed, which had been specially brought up there to give the visitors an impression of the vice-roy's magnificence.[1]

The party had hardly dined after return to their lodgings, when visitors began to pour in. Most of the Portuguese lords came to 'salute' the President and there was not a monastery in Goa which did not send its deputies to 'compliment him'. The ten days of their stay in the city were thus spent in reciprocal visits and continual feasting. One of the noblest entertainments given them was on 15 January, when they were invited by a Portuguese lord who had been Governor of Bassein and had been recently appointed to the government of Mozambique. Mandelslo's account of the feast may be quoted here:

The President overwhelmed with visits and feasts

'Every course consisted only of four dishes of meat, but they were so often changed, and the meat so excellently well dressed, that I may truly say I never was at the like. For with the meat there was brought such variety of excellent fruits that by the continual change and inter-mixture of both the appetite was sharpened and renewed. But what was most remarkable was that though the Portuguese

He is entertained by the ex-Governor of Bassein

[1] Mandelslo, op. cit., pp. 98.

ladies are as seldom seen as those of the Muscovites and Persians, yet this lord, knowing he could not in any way more oblige the English than by allowing them the sight of women, we were served at table by four handsome young maids of Malacca, while he himself was attended by two pages and an eunuch. These maids brought in the meat and filled our wine; and though he himself drunk not any, yet would he have the English treated after their own way, and drink to what height they pleased."[1]

The next day, being 16 January, the President as well as Mandelslo was invited by the Jesuits to

Invited to the New College of St. Paul

a sumptuous feast at the New College of St. Paul,[2] though our traveller may be excused for mistaking it for the Professed House of the Jesuits. The account given by Mandelslo is by far the most interesting that has been written of this college, which was perhaps the greatest and most splendid building which the Society of Jesus

[1] Mandelslo, op. cit., pp. 98–9.

[2] The New College of St. Paul, or the Convent of St. Roch, as it was generally called, was one of the finest edifices of Goa. To it was transferred, about 1610, the Old College of St. Paul which had played so conspicuous a part in the early history of the Catholic Church in the east, but which was abandoned on account of its unhealthy site. The new college was erected by the Jesuits in face of great opposition. It suffered also from successive outbreaks of fire, but the Jesuits rebuilt what was destroyed.—Tavernier, op. cit., vol. I, p. 197. Its professors were generally men of eminence from Europe. After the expulsion of the Jesuits from Goa in 1759 the college was closed, and in course of time the building fell into decay and ruin. Its materials were used for constructing the new barracks at Pangim.—Fonseca, *Sketch of the City of Goa*, pp. 315–20.

For the accounts of this college given by P. Della Valle (1623) and Dr. J. Fryer (1675) see Appendix A to this chapter.

had in the city of Goa. He testifies to the magnificence and order which prevailed in the institution under the management of the Jesuits:

'There were in this house a hundred and fifty fathers, and at least as many scholars or students, yet did not that great number fill that noble structure, which was four stories high, and had the pleasantest prospect in the world, as well towards the sea as on the land side. They first showed us all the conveniences of the house, their wealth, and the order they observed in their economy. Then they brought us into a fair arched hall, as big as an ordinary church, which was beset with tables placed all along the walls. The cloth was laid with the trenchers, the drinking cups, and earthen pots, and they had brought in bread and fruit. In the midst of the hall, there was another little square table, covered and furnished as the rest, for those who were to do penance for their having done anything contrary to the discipline of the order. In the midst of the entry to this hall there was a pillar, out of which issued a spout of water for the washing of their hands. Then they carried us up to the third storey, to another hall, which was not as large as that below, but so richly furnished as might become the apartment of a very noble house, as well in point of tapestry as other things. The table prepared for us was very large, and placed in the midst of the hall, covered with a noble cloth, beset with fruit and bread and China dishes, which persons of

Account of this famous institution

Feast given by the Jesuits

quality in those parts do prefer before those of silver. The Father Provincial having given the President the precedence sat down by him, and afterwards ordered all our company to be so placed as that between every two there were two Jesuits to entertain and discourse with us; the rest standing behind to wait on us. The meat was brought in little dishes of porcelain, to every man his own dish; and this for several courses, both of flesh and fish, all excellently well dressed. The dessert was suitable to the rest of the entertainment, and consisted in tarts, florentines, eggs dressed after the Portuguese way, admirably well perfumed, marchpains, and conserves both dry and liquid."[1]

Ball danced by Indian children who had been baptised

On rising from this sumptuous repast, the guests were conducted into several chambers where they reposed during the great heat of the day. Later on they were taken into a hall where the 'divertisement' of a ball had been arranged to entertain them, and which was danced by Indian children who had been baptised and instructed in the Roman Catholic faith. The Archbishop of Goa, who was Primate of all the Indies, was also present there, both to participate in the 'divertisement' and to entertain the President, by order of the viceroy. The ball, the details of which are given at length, being over, the guests stayed on to hear some music. On their taking leave of their hosts, the latter informed them that they made use of such amusements not

[1] Mandelslo, op. cit., p. 99.

only to induce the Hindus and Muhammadans of those parts to embrace the Christian religion but also to amuse the children who had been baptised and to give them some diversion after their studies.[1]

Invited to the Professed House by the Jesuits

On the 18th the visitors were invited to dinner by the Jesuits of the Professed House of Bom Jesus[2] which Mandelslo confuses with the College of St. Paul described above. They were received at the entrance by some of the 'most ancient' Fathers, who showed them round the halls and chambers hung with pictures of distinguished persons who had been members of their order, and who related the history of those of their society who had suffered martyrdom for the Christian religion 'among whom the authors of the Gunpowder Plot in England were not the last. But they forebore giving us the explication thereof; only they entertained us with a long relation of the cruelties, exercised some years before, upon those of their society in Japan, where the emperor had made use of the most exquisite torments (that) could be invented, upon the Christians, as well the foreigners who had spent their

[1] Mandelslo, op. cit., pp. 99–100.

[2] A Professed House is a convent or the place of abode of a fraternity that has taken the vows of some religious order.

The Professed House of the Jesuits at Goa was completed in 1589, in spite of the opposition of the Municipal Chamber of Goa and the Franciscans. The celebrated orientalist Anquetil du Perron says: 'I could not help admiring the house of the Jesuits, a superb building, which could have taken its place amongst the most beautiful Religious Buildings of Europe.'—*Zend Avesta*, traduit de A. du Perron, Paris (1771) Introduction, vol. I, p. ccxiv.

endeavours in planting religion in those parts, as upon the Japonnesses who had made profession thereof.'[1]

The Fathers next conducted the President and Mandelslo to the famous Church of Bom Jesus[2] which was attached to the house and which still remains in all its imposing splendour when so many other magnificent edifices which adorned Old Goa have long ago crumbled to pieces. Mandelslo's brief description deserves to be given:

The magnificent Church of Bom Jesus

'They brought us into the church which is no question one of the most sumptuous the Jesuits have in all Asia. The structure is vast and magnificent, and the ornaments are so suitable to the greatness thereof that it were not easy to imagine anything more noble. The first thing we were showed was the High Altar; but though it were one of the noblest I ever saw, yet came it not, in wealth, near

[1] Mandelslo, op. cit., p. 100.

[2] The stately Church of Bom Jesus at Goa was begun in 1594 and consecrated in 1605 and is still in excellent preservation, chiefly because it contains the tomb of St. Francis Xavier. The façade is an elaborate piece of workmanship and excites the admiration of the spectator. It is built of black granite and is 78 feet high and 75 feet broad. The pillars supporting the choir within bear two inscriptions, one in Latin and the other in Portuguese, recording the consecration of the church by Dom Aleixo de Menezes, Archbishop of Goa and Primate of the Indies, on 15 May, 1605. On one side of the wall is the cenotaph of Dom H. Mascarenhas, Captain of Cochin and Hormaz (Ormuz), at whose cost the church was built. The main altar contains the statue of the Infant Jesus as also another very large image of St. Ignatius Loyola, the founder of the Society of Jesus. There are two chapels, one dedicated to St. Francis Borgia, the patron saint of Portugal, and the other in honour of the immortal St. Francis Xavier, whose splendid sarcophagus it contains. —Fonseca, op. cit., pp. 283-6. See also Appendix B.

THE CHURCH OF BOM JESUS AT OLD GOA
Consecrated 15 May 1605

From Fonseca's *Sketch of the City of Goa*

another lesser one, which had been built in honour of St. Francis Xavier, whom they call the Apostle of the Indies. We were showed his image, which was upon wood, drawn according to the life, but we were told his body was still to be seen in that Church, in the same posture as it was at the time of his departure."[1] Though not specifically mentioned, Mandelslo must without doubt have seen the coffin of the saint in the famous chapel dedicated to St. Francis Xavier in this church.[2]

Mandelslo gives here the following interesting account of St. Francis Xavier whose name has become immortal in history as the 'Apostle of the Indies':

Account of the death of St. Francis Xavier

'The Jesuits told us that the body of the said Saint Francis Xavier was found in the island of Ceylon, and that it was discovered only by a most delightful smell, which had brought those

[1] Mandelslo, op. cit., p. 100.

[2] In 1624, during the solemnities at Goa connected with his canonization, the body of St. Francis Xavier was removed by the Jesuits to the Church of Bom Jesus from St. Paul's where it had been deposited after it was brought from Malacca. The ceremonies have been fully described by Della Valle who was in the city at the time. (See Appendix C.) The remains were first deposited in the Chapel of St. Francis Borgia, and later transferred to the beautiful chapel which is named after Francis Xavier. The interior of this is richly gilded and adorned with 27 choice pictures representing the life and miracles of the apostle. An altar under the arch of the chapel supports an image of the saint in solid silver four feet high gifted in 1670 by a pious Genoese lady who spent £300 on its execution. The image bears a staff in each hand, one of silver and the other of Indian cane. The latter is taken by the governors of Goa previous to assuming charge of their office, in exchange for a new one which they offer to the saint, to secure his protection over the Portuguese territories. —Fonseca, op. cit., pp. 286–9.

who had found it many leagues distance from the sea to the place where it was hidden. Which story does not agree very well with what others write of the same body. For besides that the scent which is carried from the island of Ceylon so far into the sea proceeds from the groves of cinnamon wherewith that island is in a manner covered, Maffaeus, one of the gravest authors that ever were of the Society, says in express terms that Francis Xavier, not satisfied with the progress he had made in the Indies by the means of his preaching the faith of Christ, would needs try whether it might have the like success in China, but that he died on the seaside as soon as he landed. Whereto he adds that the Master of the Ship, which had carried him thither, caused the corpse to be put into unslaked lime to the end he might carry away the bones after the flesh had been consumed; but that after certain days that consuming matter had not made any impression upon it, and that the body instead of being corrupted smelled very sweetly; and that thereupon they resolved to carry it to Goa where it was received with great ceremonies. They related to us a great many miracles wrought by that Saint; but I remember only two or three of the most considerable; to wit, that he had caused the sun to come back an hour after it was set: that he commanded the sea and the winds with the same power as our Saviour had sometimes done; and that he had raised up two men, one whereof had been buried a whole day before."[1]

[1] Mandelslo, op. cit., pp. 100–101.

After Mandelslo and the President had been shown round the great church, they were brought to the refectory, which was a large hall capable of accommodating two hundred persons at the tables placed all along the walls. At dinner only four Fathers, 'the chiefest of the order,' sat down with the guests, while all the rest stood and waited on the party. 'We were as well treated by these,' says our author 'as we had been by the others; but I must confess these gave us the best canary that ever I drunk.'[1] After it ended they were taken right up to the steeple, 'whence we could take a view of all the city, the sea, the river, and all the adjacent champion, as far as the mountain, much better than we could have done from the fourth story of the Professed House (i.e. the New College of St. Paul).'[2]

Dinner at the Professed House

[1] Mandelslo, op. cit., p. 101.

[2] St. Francis Xavier (1506–52), commonly known as the 'Apostle of the Indies', was born in Spain in the castle of Xavier at the foot of the Pyrenees. After completing his studies at the University of Paris, he joined Ignatius of Loyola and five others and established the Society of Jesus in 1534. In 1542 he arrived at Goa in charge of the mission sent by the King of Portugal to his Indian dominions, and laboured in the east for the next ten years. The work he accomplished was enormous, for he inaugurated new missionary enterprises from Ormuz to Japan. At Travancore he is said to have founded no less than forty-five Christian settlements, and he also visited Ceylon, Malacca, the Malay Archipelago and Japan. In 1552 he left Goa on a missionary enterprise to China but died of fever in the island of Chang-Chuen (St. John's) off the province of Kwang-Tung (December 2). He was buried close to the cabin in which he died. But his body was later transferred to Malacca and thence to Goa (1554) where it was deposited in St. Paul's in a crystal coffin enclosed in another of silver. In 1624 the body was removed to the Church of Bom Jesus where it still lies in a magnificent shrine. (See Appendix D.)

St. Francis Xavier was canonized by the Pope in 1621. Many mira-

The next morning two of the Fathers came to the President's lodgings and took him and his companion out to see the great hospital at Goa, of which the Jesuits were then in charge. It is described by our author as a noble structure, capable of accommodating above a thousand sick persons and fully equipped with all necessary things. The noblest apartments in the hospital were the 'kitchen' and the 'apothecary's shop' belonging to it, both well furnished. There was at the time a large number of patients in the infirmary, most of them suffering from the 'pox' or 'bloody-flux'. Those whose life was despaired of were carried to a private room where each was attended by a priest who remained there till the end came.[1]

The Royal Hospital at Goa

cles have been ascribed to him, an official list of which is preserved in the Vatican library. Though an ascetic and a mystic, to whom things spiritual were more real than the visible world, he possessed strong common sense which made him supreme as an organizer. He seems also to have had a singularly attractive personality. Not without much justice has Xavier been regarded as the greatest of Christian missionaries since the first century A.D.

For the literature on the life of St. Francis Xavier see *Ency. Brit.* (14th ed., vol. XXIII, p. 835); also Gray's note in *Pyrard de Laval*, op. cit., vol. II, p. 62.

[1] Mandelslo, op. cit., p. 101.

The Royal Hospital at Goa was a splendid institution founded by the great Albuquerque after the conquest of Goa in 1510, and it was the pride and care of successive viceroys and kings of Portugal. In 1591 its administration was placed in the hands of the Jesuits who erected a splendid building for it, and under their fostering care the hospital acquired great celebrity. The most detailed account of the institution is that given by Pyrard de Laval who was treated here in 1608. (See Appendix E.) Tavernier first visited it in 1641, only two years after Mandelslo, and again in 1648. He says that it 'was formerly renowned throughout India', but that on his second visit he found that the inmates were not well treated

The last institution among the religious edifices of Old Goa to be visited was the monastery of the Augustines which was also known under the name of the Convent of our Lady of Grace. 'It is seated,' says our traveller, 'upon a little eminency, so that seeing it at a certain distance, a man would take it for one of the noblest palaces in the world.' The friars conducted them round the building and redoubled their civilities when Mandelslo delivered to them the letters of recommendation which the Augustines at Ispahan had given to him in Persia for the purpose.

The monastery of the Augustines

(Tavernier, op. cit., vol. I, p. 198). Even in the days of its greatness, the mortality in the hospital appears to have been excessive (*Pyrard de Laval*, vol. II, p. 11). No doubt this was largely due to cholera, scurvy, enteric and venereal diseases with which the science of the time was not able to deal. The practice of bleeding patients as often as thirty or forty times had also something to do with this heavy toll of life (Fryer, *East India and Persia*, Hakluyt Society (1909–12) vol. II, p. 14). The hospital was intended only for soldiers and for such as had no home in the city. See also Fonseca, op. cit., pp. 228–36.

CHAPTER VIII

MANDELSLO'S GENERAL ACCOUNT OF THE PORTUGUESE IN GOA

Methwold takes leave of his hosts who send him large presents

PRESIDENT METHWOLD at last completed his business with the viceroy who paid him nine thousand pounds sterling in ready money, and promised that the rest would be paid, either in money or in commodities, to those English merchants whom the President had for that purpose brought with him from Surat. Methwold now took leave of all those whose civilities he had received. The viceroy, the general of the galleons, and the principal lords about the court sent him very considerable presents. The viceroy presented him with several skins of cinnamon, a biggel,[1] some butts of sack, sheep and baskets of fruit. The Jesuits sent him aquavitae,[2] a good store of all sorts of conserves, dry and liquid, and requested that he would take along with him to England certain Jesuits, one of whom had lived long enough in China to be thoroughly acquainted with that country.

[1] The biggel is apparently the *nilgau* or blue cow. Mandelslo says that with the horses in the viceroy's establishment at Goa he saw a biggel, 'which is a creature about the bigness and much the same colour as a *renne*, but is headed like a horse, maned like an ass, having black and cloven feet, and upon his head two black horns.'—Mandelslo, op. cit., p. 98.

[2] Aquavitae (*L.* water of life) any form of ardent spirits such as brandy, whisky, etc.

Mandelslo's *Travels* refer to a very important topical episode at the time of his arrival at Goa, namely, the fact of the port being then under a formal blockade imposed by a dozen Dutch ships. This was the very period when Portuguese supremacy at sea and their possessions in the east were challenged by this energetic Protestant nation ; and throughout the first half of the seventeenth century the power of the former was on the decline.[1] The blockade by the Hollanders, however, could only prevent the galleons and the carracks[2] from leaving the harbour, for Mandelslo saw one day about three hundred frigates and boats enter the port and proceed up the river to the city laden with all sorts of provisions and commodities such as pepper, ginger, cardamon, sugar, rice, fruits and conserves.[3]

Blockade of Goa by the Dutch in January, 1639

On 20 January 1639, the President and his party left the city of Goa by the river, and as soon as they got out of it they made for the general's galleon which was called the *Bom Jesus* and which is described as 'one of the noblest vessels I ever saw', for it

Final visit to the General of the Galleons

[1] 'Before the Dutch had beaten down the power of the Portuguese in India, one saw at Goa nothing but magnificence and wealth, but since these late comers have deprived them of their trade in all directions, they have lost the sources of their gold and silver, and are altogether come down from their former splendour.'—Tavernier, *Travels in India*, translated by Ball, London (1889) vol. I p. 187.

[2] 'These carracks are ordinarily of 1,500 to 2,000 tons' burthen, sometimes more, so that they are the largest vessels in the world ; they cannot float in less than ten fathoms of water.'—*Voyage of Pyrard de Laval*, translated by Gray and Bell, Hakluyt Society (1887) vol. II, p. 181.

[3] Mandelslo, op. cit., pp. 98, 102.

carried 60 brass guns, all cannon or culverings, with 600 men, mariners and soldiers, on board:

'The general received the President with much civility, and brought him into his chamber, and after a collation of conserves and sack, contrary to the custom of the Portuguese, who never proffer a man drink unless he ask for it, he showed us all the ship, which had the name of a galleon, but might very well be accounted a carrack by reason of the bigness of it. The other vessels of the fleet were also very noble ones, there being not any one among them that had not fifty guns at least.'[1]

The President at last took leave and came on board the *Mary* to the booming of guns from the Portuguese fleet, and his ship took up a position in the roadstead between the two hostile fleets. After two days, on the 22nd, Methwold dismissed the two ships that had come with him from Surat and which were to carry thither the money that had been received at Goa.[2] The admiral in charge of the Dutch fleet, whose name is given as Van Keulen,[3] was expected to pay him a visit in view of the fact that he had

Departure from Goa, 23 January 1639

[1] Mandelslo, op. cit., p. 102.

[2] Two ships, the *Blessing* and the *Michael*, had accompanied the *Mary* from Surat to Goa. The former was old and worn out and it was intended to sell her to the Portuguese. The pinnace *Michael* was to bring back the crew of the *Blessing* and also Cogan and Wylde, two members of the Surat council, who had accompanied the ex-President Methwold to Goa to receive the money promised by the viceroy and to assist in the disposal of the other ship.—*English Factories in India* (1637–41) edited by Foster pp. 88, 118–9.

[3] The name is Antonio Caen according to the *Hague Transcripts*, series I, vol. XI, nos. 350, 358, 360.

requested the President to convey some of his letters to his superiors in Europe. But finding at last that the Dutch fleet had sailed away in the direction of Ceylon, Methwold gave orders to proceed on the voyage.[1]

Mandelslo at this stage devotes several pages to a general account of the city of Goa,[2] including its topography, its Portuguese inhabitants, the habits of their women, the life of Hindus and Muslims of this place, the court, the powers of the viceroys and other topics. We shall very briefly review this account, indicating some of the interesting features of the life of the people and the character of the government.

General account of Goa and Portuguese India

The name of the viceroy at Goa at the time of Mandelslo's visit was Dom Pedro da Silva, but we are told that his person was not in conformity with his high position.[3] He had about him a court of more than fifty gentle-

The viceroys of Goa

[1] Mandelslo, op. cit., p. 108.

[2] Dr. J. Fryer (1675) says: 'The city is a Rome in India, both for absoluteness and fabrics, the chiefest consisting of churches, and convents, or religious houses.'—*East India and Persia*, Hakluyt Society (1909–12) vol. II, p. 26.

[3] One of the best accounts of the viceroys of Portuguese India, their court, their magnificence and their government is given by Pyrard de Laval, op. cit., vol. II, p. 76–88. For example:

'The viceroy treats none with familiarity, nor ever goes to assemblies or banquets. He goes abroad but rarely, except on the great festivals. On the evening preceding the day when he intends to go forth, drums and trumpets are sounded throughout the whole town as a warning to the nobility, who assemble in the early morning before the palace, all on horseback and in grand array.'—pp. 78–9.

men who gave him the same respect that was due to the king in Europe. The viceroy was changed about every three years: partly because the king thought it unsafe to allow a subject to hold such a dignity for long, and also because the King of Spain desired to distribute his patronage among a large number of his nobles so as to enable them to amass a fortune in a short period.[1] This was possible because the court of the viceroy at Goa was maintained at the king's expense and also because the disposal of all the revenues was left in his hands. Every year the viceroy made an extensive tour over the territories under his control, and this brought him a large sum of money by way of presents from the neighbouring princes and from the governors and other subordinate officers.[2] The viceroy was supreme civil and criminal judge and only in rare cases was an

[1] 'This frequent change of viceroys is displeasing to the Portuguese and to the Indians as is no less that of the governors of the various forts and other officers. To illustrate which they tell a parable, how that one day there lay a poor man at the door of a church, his legs full of ulcers, and so covered with flies as was pitiful to behold; up came a neighbour who, thinking to do him a kindness, drove away the flies: whereat the poor patient was much vexed, saying that the flies he drove away already had their bellies full, and would not bite him more, whereas those that would come would be hungry and would sting him worse. So it is, they say, with the viceroys, for the gorged depart and the hungry arrive.' —*Pyrard de Laval*, op. cit., vol. II, p. 87.

[2] Tavernier says: 'It was formerly one of the most splendid posts in the world for a noble to be viceroy of Goa, and there are few monarchs who are able to bestow governments worth so much as are those which depend upon this viceroy.'—op. cit., vol. I, p. 190. These governors, who were appointed by the viceroy, also held office for three years. There were five of them in charge respectively of Mozambique, Malacca, Hormaz, Muscat and Ceylon. Besides these the viceroy had the patronage of a number of high offices in Goa and other places.

appeal allowed to the king. At his arrival in the Indies a new viceroy used generally to land at the island of Bardes, to the north of the capital, from which place he sent his agents to Goa to take possession of the new charge and all its appurtenances. His predecessor made way for him on the first news of his arrival, unfurnished the palace, and left him only the guards and the bare walls.[1]

The Castiços and the Mestiços

The Portuguese inhabitants of Goa are described as falling into two classes: the Castiços, born of Portuguese parents; and Mestiços, born of a Portuguese father and an Indian mother.[2] The latter were distinguished by their olive colour, and those of the third generation were as dark as the natives of the country. Persons of quality never went abroad on foot; but were either carried about in a palankeen by their slaves, or rode on horseback or went in gilt and painted gondolas. They were always attended by a slave who carried a fan or an umbrella. The Portuguese, says Mandelslo, had the reputation of being highly conceited of themselves; but those of Goa were prouder in their gait and actions than any others of their nationality.[3] They were also

[1] Mandelslo, op. cit., p. 108.

[2] 'The Portuguese, whether of Europe or Brazil, are at Goa called indifferently *Frangues* or *Fringuins*; those born in India of pure Portuguese blood, Castiços, corresponding to the *Creoles* of America; half-castes are *Mestiços*.' —*Pyrard de Laval*, op. cit., vol. II, p. 38 *n*.

[3] 'The Portuguese who go to India have no sooner passed the Cape of Good Hope than they all become *Fidalgos* or gentlemen, and add *Dom* to the simple name of Pedro or Jeronimo which they carried when they embarked; this is the reason why they are commonly called in derision 'Fidalgos of the Cape of Good Hope.'—Tavernier, op. cit., vol. I, p. 188.

most punctilious and 'excessively civil one to another' in their social life.[1]

Mandelslo's account of the dress and habits of the Portuguese women at Goa is interesting. His reference to the decay of Portuguese morals, both among the men and women, and the general corruption of society, is amply confirmed by the French traveller Pyrard de Laval who resided in Goa for twenty months some thirty years before the visit of the German traveller. This social decline has generally been acknowledged by historians to form, along with the implacable hostility of the Dutch and the devastating effects of successive epidemics, one of the causes of the decline and fall of Portuguese greatness in the east.[2]

Decline of Portuguese morals

'There are few Portuguese women or Mestiços,' says Mandelslo, 'seen going about the city; and when they go abroad, either to church or upon necessary visits, they are carried in close palankeens or are attended and watched by so many slaves that it is impossible to speak to them. When they appear in public, they are all very richly attired in velvet, flowered satin, or brocado, and adorned with abundance of pearls and precious stones;[3] but at

Dress and manners of their women

[1] Mandelslo, op. cit., p. 103.

[2] For other causes see H. Heras, 'The Decay of the Portuguese in India', *Journal of the Bombay Historical Society*, 1928, vol. I, pp. 36–41.

[3] 'The rich ladies of quality go but seldom to church, save on the great feast days, and then superbly attired in the Portuguese mode. Their gowns for the most part are of gold, silk, and silver brocade, enriched with

home they go in their hair, and have about them only a smock which reaches to the navel; and thence downwards they have petticoats of painted cloths falling down to the feet, which are bare.[1] They eat no bread, as liking the rice better, now that they are accustomed to it; nor do they fare over-deliciously as to other things, their ordinary sustenance being salt fish, mangas,[2] or only rice soaked in a little flesh or fish-broth. They make use of certain bottles made of a kind of black earth, which they call gorgolettes,[3] and have a pipe coming up to the brims so that they may suck up the water without lifting up the bottles to their mouths.'[4]

The corruption of morals was perhaps the most

pearls, gems and jewels at the head, arms, hands, and waist. Over all they wear a veil of the finest crape in the world, reaching from the head to the foot. They never wear stockings. Their pattens, or *chapins*, are open above, and cover only the soles of the feet; but they are all broidered with gold and silver, hammered in thin plates which reach over the lower surface of the *chapin*, the upper part being covered with pearls and gems and the soles half a foot thick with cork.'—*Pyrard de Laval*, op. cit., vol. II, p. 102.

[1] 'The women take their ease in their smocks or *bajus*, which are more transparent and fine than the most delicate crape of these parts; so that their skin shows beneath as clearly as if they had nothing on; more than that, they expose the bosom to such an extent that one can see quite down to the waist.'—*Pyrard de Laval*, op. cit., vol. II, p. 112.

[2] *Mangas de velludo* (Port. = velvet sleeves) are a kind of sea-mew, white all over the body and having black wings. Mandelslo, op. cit., p. 248.

[3] *Gorgoleta* (Port.) are earthen and narrow-mouthed vessels for storing drinking water. They are so called from the gurgling sound that is made when water is poured out of them into the mouth from a distance, so as to avoid contact. The word is still current under the form of 'goglet'. The Indians call it *kunja*.—*Pyrard de Laval*, op. cit., vol. I, p. 329 *n*; vol. II, p. 74; Fryer, op. cit., vol. I, p. 125.

[4] Mandelslo, op. cit., p. 105.

serious canker in Portuguese society at Goa during the first half of the seventeenth century, and the reference to it may be given here:

'The men there are so jealous of their wives that they permit not their nearest relations to see them:[1] for chastity is so strange a virtue in those parts, that there is no woman but contrives all the ways imaginable to pursue her enjoyments, never minding the breach of those laws which God and nature hath imposed upon them, though the frequent misfortunes which happen upon that occasion should engage them to be more cautious and reserved. The perpetual idle life they lead makes them so high in their desires for they do not anything of business in the world but spend the day in chewing of beetle, which adds fuel to the flames, as do also the cloves and nutmegs which they eat out of an imagination that they prevent the corruptions of the teeth and stomach, which commonly make the breath stink.'[2]

Employment of slaves

Slavery appears to have been an accepted institution in Portuguese India, though there is no evidence to show that

[1] Fryer says: 'They being jealous of their honour, pardon no affront; wherefore to ogle a lady in a balcony (if a person of quality) it is revenged with a bocca mortis' (Port. *bacamarte* = a blunderbuss).—op. cit., vol. II, p. 26. So also Tavernier: 'It may be said that the Portuguese dwelling in India are the most vindictive and the most jealous of their women of all the people in the world.'—op. cit., vol. I, p. 188.

[2] Mandelslo, op. cit., p. 105. cf. *Pyrard de Laval*, op. cit., vol. II, pp. 113–14; Fonseca, *Sketch of the City of Goa*, pp. 161–2; *Voyage of J. Huyghen van Linschoten*, edited by Burnell and Tiele, Hakluyt Society, (1885) vol. I, pp. 208–14.

the masters were inhuman in their treatment of this unfortunate class:

'Most of the Portuguese,' says our traveller, have many slaves of both sexes,[1] whom they employ not only about their persons, but also upon any other business they are capable of, for what they get comes in to the master. Whence it comes that handsome wenches are sought after, to be employed in the selling of fruits and such commodities as the Portuguese send to market, to the end their beauty might draw in customers. Their keeping, as to diet, stands them in very little. The children born between slaves belong to the master, unless the father will redeem them within eight or ten days after they are born.'[2]

Goa an emporium of trade

The old city of Goa still maintained its position as the centre of a very flourishing trade which was carried on by the Portuguese with Bengal, Pegu, Malacca, China and Gujarat:

'No person of quality at Goa but goes once a day to the market, whither the merchants, nay most gentlemen come, as well to hear what news there is, as to see what there is to be sold; for, from 7 in the morning to 9 (after which the heat is such as

[1] Pyrard de Laval gives a good account of the sale of slaves in the market-place at Goa. 'In this place are to be seen numbers of slaves whom they drive there as we do horses here; and you see that sellers come with great troops following.'—op. cit., vol. II, pp. 65–6. Again, 'As for the slaves of Goa, their number is infinite; they are of all the Indian nations, and a very great traffic is done in them. They are exported to Portugal and to all places under the Portuguese dominion.'—ibid., p. 39.

[2] Mandelslo, op. cit., pp. 105–6.

7

that a man is not able to stay there) the public criers, whom they call *laylon*, sell there by outcry all sorts of commodities, but especially slaves of both sexes and jewels . . . There are also to be sold there Persian and Arabian horses, spices, all sorts of aromatic gums, alcatifs, porcelain, vessels of agate, several things made of lacque, and whatever is thought precious or rare in any other part of the Indies. Merchants and tradesmen are distinguished by streets; so that silkmen are not shuffled in among linen drapers, nor the druggists among those who sell porcelain. The greatest profit they make is in the exchange of money."[1]

The Hindu population

In the account of the Hindu residents of Goa, one point deserving notice is that there were among them several able physicians who were so highly respected at Goa that they were permitted to have their umbrellas carried with them, a privilege which was extended only to persons of quality. We are also told that the Portuguese, and even the viceroy and the archbishop, requisitioned the service of these physicians in preference to those of their own nation.

[1] The principal thoroughfare and business centre at Goa was the *Rua Direita*, or the Straight Avenue, which was lined on both sides by fine buildings where lapidaries, goldsmiths, bankers and all the leading merchants and artisans at Goa carried on their business. There were Portuguese, Germans, Italians, etc. The locality was densely thronged by people who attended auction sales held there from morning to noon.—Fonseca, op. cit., p. 198. Mandelslo says that the public criers were called *laylon*, while Pyrard (op. cit., vol. II, p. 52) gives this name to the locality. The Portuguese word *leilao* = auction is oriental in origin, being derived from the Arabic *i'lam* = proclamation or advertisement.

With the above survey of Mandelslo's account of the city and people of Goa, we shall resume our sketch of his voyage. On 22 January his ship crossed Goa bar and, sailing along the Malabar coast, reached the island of Ceylon on the 29th. Here, says our author, 'we were fixed as immovable by a calm which lasted three weeks complete,' and it was not till 20 February that the *Mary* was in a position, on account of favourable winds, to proceed on her voyage across the Indian Ocean towards the coast of South Africa.

Arrival at Ceylon

At this stage the work which goes under Mandelslo's name enters into a long and elaborate digression concerning the countries of the Far East, namely Pegu, Siam, Cambodia, Java, Amboyna, the Phillipines, Japan and China. This covers no less than 127 pages of the English folio edition,[1] with closely printed matter, and forms more than one-third of the work. Practically the whole of the second of the three books in which his voyages and travels are treated is devoted to the above-mentioned countries. In view of the fact that Mandelslo never went beyond Ceylon, and never visited any of these eastern islands and kingdoms, it is conclusive that the account is the work of his French translator, as stated in Davies' Introduction.

Interpolation on the countries of the Far East

In the light of the conclusion mentioned above, it is interesting to note the following passage which appears to have been specially inserted by the

[1] Namely, pp. 115–242.

French translator, A. de Wicquefort, to put the reader under the impression that the account of these Far-Eastern lands was derived by Mandelslo from the Jesuits on board his ship:

'The calm stayed our ship hard by this isle (Ceylon) for near upon three weeks, which I employed in enquiring of our President and certain Jesuits, who were aboard our vessels, into this pleasant part of the Indies which I had never seen, and merits to be known by the Description I shall make from the report of these persons amongst whom there were some who had spent there the best part of their lives. I will then begin with the place where we were, and faithfully deliver you all I could learn of those kingdoms and provinces which without question are the wealthiest of any in the world."[1]

[1] Mandelslo, op. cit., pp. 115–6.

CHAPTER IX

MANDELSLO'S VOYAGE FROM CEYLON TO THE ENGLISH CHANNEL

Plan of the rest of the work

HAVING so closely followed our interesting traveller through the cities of western India, the reader must naturally wish to have some information about the last period of Mandelslo's travels after he left the Indian peninsula. We propose, therefore, to devote this chapter to a summary of his long voyage to Europe, and shall reserve the last chapter for an account of his stay in England as a guest of the English President and his journey across the Netherlands to his home in north Germany, which he reached on 1 May 1640.

The *Mary* crosses the Indian Ocean to the Cape

After the three weeks' enforced stay off the island of Ceylon, the *Mary*, taking advantage of the north-west wind, directed her course across the Indian Ocean for the voyage homewards on 20 February 1639. A month later, in mid-ocean, the action of a butler, who set fire to a vat which he had filled with aquavitae, nearly caused the ruin of the ship, as it was laden with all sorts of gums and other fatty drugs; the fire was however smothered before it could spread. Passing by Maurice Island[1]

[1] This is Mauritius, named by the Dutch Maurice Island, 'from the Prince of Orange who was Admiral of the United Provinces at the

the ship reached the south coast of Africa, and, rounding the Cape d'Agulhas and the False Cape, arrived at the Cape of Good Hope on 5 May. Mandelslo gives an account of the savage inhabitants (Hottentots) of this part of Africa who lived on dead animals and dead whales cast up by the sea on the shore, who knew neither God nor the devil, and whose only enemies were the lions.[1]

The further progress of the vessel was now hindered by very tempestuous weather and a succession of terrific hurricanes which nearly wrecked the ship, and which decided the captain and the President to divert their course and proceed to the island of Madagascar, there to pass the monsoon until the seas were calm, and also to refit the vessel with the necessary water and provisions. Mandelslo's account of the situation deserves to be quoted:

Terrible storms at the Cape of Good Hope

'May 26. The wind increased so by degrees that we were forced to take in all but the main sail, which was not taken in till the wind grew so violent as if it would have confounded all the elements, to swallow us up in the disaster. Nay its fury was such that our ship, which had resisted all before as a rock, was tossed by the waves like a little boat. I must confess it was through God's infinite mercy to us that we escaped that danger, wherein we were in

time of their first voyage into the Indies.'—Mandelslo, op. cit., p. 246. Maurice of Nassau, Prince of Orange (1567–1625) was the second son of William the Silent, and became Stadtholder of Holland and Zeeland on his father's assassination in 1584.

[1] Mandelslo, op. cit., p. 250.

all likelihood to perish, since it was a kind of miracle that the masts stood, considering the violence of the winds was such as might have rooted up the strongest trees.'[1]

On the way to Madagascar the fact is recorded that on Whit Sunday a tiger cub which had been brought from Surat bit the President in the hand and would have wrenched it off had not Mandelslo and others come to timely assistance.[2] On 2 July, the ship reached Madagascar and cast anchor in the Bay of St. Augustine. Here it remained for over six weeks after which it resumed its voyage back to the Cape. The President had a tent pitched for himself by the seaside, and huts were put up for the soldiers and others who carried out certain repairs on the land, as also for the butchers who killed and salted the beef for the provision of the ship. But on Sundays all came on board, where a sermon was given.

The ship arrives at Madagascar

By a happy coincidence the President had the pleasure of meeting at this place three other English vessels. One of these was encountered a week before the arrival at the island. It was of 500 tons' burden, belonged to the new Company and was under the command of Captain Hall. It had left England some four months before and was bound for the Indies. The other two vessels were found at anchor

Meets with other English vessels at this island

[1] Mandelslo, op. cit., p. 251.

[2] The tiger cub was probably intended for a present to King Charles I; but having proved vicious on the voyage it had to be destroyed. —*English Factories in India* (1637–41) edited by Foster, p. xv.

in the bay, both of them belonging to the old company: one of these, called the *London*, was a large ship of 1,400 tons, commanded by Captain Willis. All the captains offered to supply the President with cordage and sails and other things necessary for the prosecution of his voyage. Methwold invited them and the officers of the ships to dinner. Some days later, Captain Willis treated the whole company, and entertained it with a comedy which lasted about three hours. After some ten days, the two ships bound for India left the island.[1]

Mandelslo gives a lively account of his stay at the island of Madagascar.[2] One of the chiefs

Barter of goods with the people of the place

of these parts came over to see him accompanied by his three sons with a retinue of about a hundred men armed with pikes. The eldest of the three brothers presented the President with twelve goats and each of his two wives gave a fat capon. In return Methwold offered him three strings of glass coral, each of his brothers two, and each of the wives a bracelet. Their value was insignificant but the recipients valued them highly. They planted a great pole in the ground as a mark of the alliance, and having asked to hear English music were much pleased with it. Then followed some exchange of commodities on the basis of truck or barter. A fat

[1] The *London* anchored in 'Swally Hole' at Surat on September 20, 1639 'with her people all in good health'.—*English Factories in India* (1637–41) edited by Foster, p. 194.

[2] An interpolation on the history and inhabitants of Madagascar covers pp. 254–8 of the English (1662) edition.

sheep, the tail whereof weighed 20 or 24 pounds, was bought for seven or eight grains of coral or agate, and a capon for three or four grains of counterfeit coral. 'They would not,' says our traveller, 'meddle with our money, as being so happy as not to know the value of a thing which occasions the misery of other parts of the world.'[1] Some time before this four oxen had been purchased for forty pairs of glass bracelets, a sheep for two, and a calf for three; and 'for a brass ring, ten or twelve inches about, a man might have an ox worth six or seven pounds'.

After over six weeks' stay at Madagascar, the President's ship left the island on 21 August to prosecute her voyage, after having purchased from the native chiefs of the place 25 fat oxen and about 100 sheep and goats, in addition to the 150 oxen which had been bought during their abode on the island, so that the ship might not be in want of fresh meat during the remainder of the voyage. The *Mary* now proceeded with a favourable wind and, rounding the Cape further south than before, at last reached the island of St. Helena on 6 October, this being the place at which every East Indiaman used to touch.[2] The description of the place by Mandelslo's editor gives a very favourable idea of the island. 'At this place,'

Resumption of the voyage to the Cape

[1] Mandelslo, op. cit., p. 254.

[2] Mandelslo, or rather his editor, leaves us under the impression that the ship actually touched at St. Helena. But the log of the *Mary* says very definitely that 'finding that they had shot past the island, they resumed the voyage'. (See Appendix to this chapter.) There is a slight discrepancy in the dates mentioned.

he says, 'a man may have at any time of the year figs, pomegranates, citrons and oranges, and there are goats, swine, barbary hens, pheasants, partridges, quails, peacocks, pigeons, and great store of all sorts of birds, and also salt for the keeping of them; so that the ships might be sufficiently provided with all things if they would stay there any time. The sea supplies it with more fish than can be consumed, and the earth brings forth so many excellent herbs that the Portuguese, unwilling to retard their voyage, leave at this place their sick men who recover their health within a few days, and having only a little oil, rice, bisket and spice, make a shift to live there till the ships come thither the next year.'[1]

The island of St. Helena

Though Mandelslo's ship, being now well provided with water and provisions, did not touch at the islands of Ascension and St. Thomas, or at Cape Verde, we find these places carefully described in his work. So also is there a very long interpolation about the history, manners and customs of the people inhabiting the Guinea coast, the Kingdom of the Congo and the Canary Islands.[2] There is little doubt that all this elaborate disquisition is from the pen of the 'learned' Olearius, or more probably from that of the French editor De Wicquefort, for we come across in these digressions such dates as 6 May 1642,[3] which are later than the end of Mandelslo's travels.

Digressions

[1] Mandelslo, op. cit., p. 261. [2] ibid., pp. 264–71, 273–8.
[3] ibid., p. 273.

Arrival on the coast of England

After passing Cape Verde on 3 November, the ship sailed past the island of Flores near the Azores Archipelago in the north Atlantic on the 29th of the same month. On 11 December the *Mary* sighted Land's End, at the extreme end of the county of Cornwall, and entered the English Channel. The long voyage ended on 16 December 1639, when the *Mary* passed in sight of Dover Castle and at noon came to the Downs. 'We cast anchor here,' says our author 'near three men-of-war which lay at anchor in the same road; and thus we completed our voyage in the 12th month after our departure from Surat.'[1]

[1] Mandelslo, op. cit., p. 279.

CHAPTER X

MANDELSLO'S ARRIVAL IN ENGLAND AND THE LAST DAYS OF HIS TRAVELS

THERE were over a hundred vessels lying at anchor in the Downs when Mandelslo and the English President arrived there at the end of their long journey, nearly twelve months after their departure from Surat. The lord admiral, who commanded the men-of-war, sent his shallop to congratulate the President on his safe return. On the 19th he invited Methwold to dinner, and Mandelslo, who accompanied him, expresses his surprise at the 'prodigious quantity of silver plate' and the sumptuously furnished table. After dinner they had no sooner entered their boat to return than a great tempest arose and it was impossible to reach their ship, which was not more than a musket-shot from the admiral's. It was a terrible night, and all in the boat were in water up to the waist when, after four hours' tossing about, they discovered and entered a small vessel which had lost all its anchors but one. This proved hardly more safe than the boat they had left, but they held on grimly until the next morning when, the tempest having subsided, they were brought to their own ship more than half dead from fright and fatigue. 'We were received,' says

Mandelslo and the President nearly drowned in the Downs during a tempest

Mandelslo, 'as persons risen from the dead, inasmuch as all who had seen our boat carried away by the violence of the winds had given us over for irrecoverably lost; nay, so far did they despair of ever seeing us again, that they had already bewailed our death.'[1]

Arrival in London where the President receives a warm welcome

Mandelslo and the President went on shore on 26 December and reached the cathedral town of Canterbury the same night. Passing by Gravesend they reached London on the 28th, and here certain deputies of the East India Company awaited the President's arrival in eight coaches at Blackwall. With them came Methwold's wife whom her husband had not seen for seven years. The President would needs have Mandelslo salute her in the English way and at the same time invited him to his home as his guest, there to participate in the honours done him on his arrival. On 30 December our traveller visited the East India House and personally thanked the officers there for the civilities he had received from the President.[2] On 2 January 1640, the Lord Mayor of London invited both and they had a long conversation, the former recounting stories of hardships and sufferings at sea far greater

[1] Mandelslo, op. cit., p. 279.

[2] On Mandelslo's arrival in England the Company at first decided to make him pay for his passage, the decision on this point having been left to it by the Surat authorities. (See p. 56 *n*.) But afterwards, at Methwold's suggestion, this claim was relinquished: whereupon Mandelslo gave £5 to the poor-box in acknowledgement of the Company's kindness.—*English Factories in India* (1637–41) edited by Foster, p. 118 *n*.

than any encountered by his guests on their long voyage.[1]

A few days later, Mandelslo had the honour of being presented to His Majesty King Charles I on the eve of the outbreak of that momentous Revolution which was to cost the latter both his crown and his life. 'The sixth of January (1640),' says our traveller, 'being Twelfth-day, the King of England touched many that were troubled with the Evil.[2] That ceremony ended, my Lord Strafford brought me to His Majesty who was pleased to honour me with the kissing of his hand. The next day the same lord procured me the like honour from the Queen; besides which he did me several other extraordinary favours upon all occasions. Afterwards I went often to court, where Their Majesties were pleased I should entertain them with some particulars of my Travels, especially as to what I had observed in Muscovy and Persia.'[3]

Mandelslo presented to King Charles I and the Queen

Mandelslo's stay in London was prolonged for three months partly to refresh him from the effects of the long voyage home, as also in expectation of some money from his Prince, the Duke of Holstein, to enable him to requite his obligations to those who had treated him so kindly from the date of his

He stays in London for three months

[1] Mandelslo, op. cit., p. 280.

[2] i.e., the king's evil or scrofula. The royal touch was supposed to cure the disease. The king gave a gold coin to those touched by him for 'the evil'.

[3] Mandelslo, op. cit., p. 283.

arrival at Surat to that time, and to furnish him with the means of returning to his own country. These months were pleasantly spent in attending the court where he had made several acquaintances and in visiting the public and private structures of the famous city, such as Whitehall, St. James's, Hampton Court, Windsor, Westminster Hall, the Abbey, the Tower and Greenwich.

Mandelslo at last left London on 20 March 1640 for the Low Countries on his way to his native land.

Passes through the Netherlands on his way to Holstein

Crossing the Channel from Dover to Dunkirk he travelled by easy stages through the Duchies of Flanders and Brabant by way of Bruges, Ghent, Brussels, Louvain and Antwerp. Entering the United Provinces of Holland his route lay through Breda, Gertrudenberg, Rotterdam, The Hague and Leyden to Haarlem, which was then the biggest town in Holland after the capital and is famous for the invention of printing in 1420–40. On 15 April, Mandelslo entered the great emporium of Amsterdam, having taken over three weeks since leaving London.

Holland was during the first half of the seventeenth century one of the great powers of

His account of the splendour of Amsterdam in 1640

Europe and the Dutch nation had at this period secured the monopoly of the carrying trade of the world. Under these circumstances there were few capitals in Europe that could rival Amsterdam in population, wealth and commercial activity.

Mandelslo, during his stay in the Indies, had heard much about the greatness of this capital, but what he saw now far surpassed his expectations, and he gives a long account of it in his *Travels*. The Exchanges at London and Antwerp, he tells us, were indeed noble places; but that of Amsterdam far surpassed the other two in regard to the number of merchants daily resorting there at noon.[1] It seemed to him that 'the East and the North had brought thither all their commodities, whereof there were in the shops but the patterns, whereas the main stock was disposed into store-houses, public weighing places, sledges in the streets, the quays and the flat-bottomed boats which unload the great ships.'[2]

All-round greatness of the Dutch capital

Our traveller was so struck with the splendour and wealth of the Dutch capital that he was at a loss to decide what he should admire most in that great city: whether its commerce which was greater than that of all the other cities of the Low Countries put together; or the neatness and the 'sweetness' of its streets; or the magnificence of its public and private buildings; or the largeness of its port wherein seven or eight hundred ships lay at anchor at all times; or the order and policy observed by its 'Magistrate' in all things relating to the trade and welfare of the city.

Mandelslo especially refers to the headquarters of the Dutch East India Company in Amsterdam.

[1] Mandelslo, op. cit., p. 286. [2] ibid., p. 284.

'When I saw,' he says, 'the storehouses and magazines, reaching at a great distance from the East India House, full of spices, silks, stuffs, porcelain and whatever China and the Indies afford that is most rare, I thought Ceylon had sent thither all its cinnamon, the Moluccas all their cloves, the Islands of Sumatra and Java all their spices, China all its rich stuffs, Japan its excellent works of several kinds, and the rest of the Indies its pepper and silk.'[1]

Dutch East India House described

After a week's stay at Amsterdam, Mandelslo took ship on 23 April for Hamburg which he reached five days later. After resting in that town for a day, he arrived on 1 May 1640 at Gottorp in Holstein which was his destination, and presented himself before Their Highnesses the Duke and Duchess of Holstein, 'and so put a period to my long and toilsome Travels.'

Arrival at Gottorp in Holstein

We thus take leave of Mandelslo, a cultured and gallant gentleman, possessed of prudence and discretion beyond his years, and ready to appreciate the life and character of the eastern people among whom he had travelled. A close study of his diary makes us endorse without hesitation the glowing testimonial given to him by the President and council at Surat when they describe him as 'the civillest, modestest, and fairest behaved (gentleman) that we have ever known of his age and education.'[2]

Character of Mandelslo

[1] Mandelslo, op. cit., p. 285.

[2] *English Factories in India* (1637-41) edited by Foster, p. 118.

8

It was not to be expected that after such an active and adventurous career in so many distant countries of the world, Mandelslo would be satisfied with a humdrum life in a small provincial town in the north of Germany. We can, however, gather little about his further career in Europe except the following record by John Davies of Kidwelly in his preface to the English translation of Olearius published in 1662:

Later career and death

'Mandelslo . . . left the court of Holstein, where he found not employment proportionable to his merit, and, betaking himself to another profession, he got into a regiment of horse, commanded by a German, who, purely by his military accomplishments, had raised himself to one of the greatest dignities of France.[1] He had therein the command

[1] This was Josias, Comte de Rantzau, a German by nationality, who entered the military service of France in 1635 under Richelieu and soon rose to the dignity of Marshal of France. He was a native of Holstein, a fact which explains why Mandelslo came to attach himself to his regiment on his return from his eastern travels. Marshal Rantzau was a man of great courage (he lost an eye and a foot in the wars), and his considerable military gifts, coupled with an impressive appearance, made him a favourite at the French court, which after 1642 was under the influence of Cardinal Mazarin. He served under the great Condé in the final stage of the Thirty Years' War; took a leading part in the capture of Dunkirk from Spain (1646) and was in charge of the 'Army of Flanders' (1647). In 1650 he was disgraced and imprisoned in the fortress of Vincennes on an accusation of secret dealings with the Spaniards. Prince Condé and the Marshal were often on bad turns partly owing to the latter's temper and his inveterate habit of hard drinking, in connexion with which an interesting story is recorded. When in 1639, in the early years of his service in France, an insurrection broke out at Rouen in Normandy owing to increased royal imposts, there was hesitation in the council of King Louis XIII in choosing between Marshal Rantzau and M. de Gassion to

of a troop, and, being a person of much courage, and endued with all the qualities requisite to the making of a great man, was likely to have raised himself to a more than ordinary fortune when, coming to Paris to pass away the winter, he there died of the smallpox.'[1]

command the forces ordered to march into Normandy. 'That country yields no wine,' said the King: 'that will not do for Rantzau, or be good quarters for him.' And so Gassion, who was not so heavy a drinker as Rantzau, was sent.—E. Godley, *The Great Condé*, pp. 80-81, 171, 173, 202; Guizot, *History of France*, translated by R. Black, vol. IV, p. 83.

[1] *Olearius' Voyages and Travels of the Ambassadors*, translated by J. Davies, London (1662) Preface.

APPENDIX TO CHAPTER III

SHANTIDAS JHAVERI'S JAIN TEMPLE OF CHINTAMANI IN SARASPUR AT AHMADABAD

Mandelslo's detailed account given in Chapter III is the most complete description yet available of this famous temple and it is, therefore, of great importance. The temple was built in 1622, during the reign of the Emperor Jahangir, by Shantidas Jhaveri, the foremost jeweller and banker in Gujarat in the first half of the seventeenth century. Shantidas stood in high favour at the courts of Jahangir and Shah Jahan, where he was an honoured guest, and, according to historical tradition, he received from the former the title of Nagarsheth or Lord Mayor of Ahmadabad, which his descendants enjoy till this day. The temple was dedicated to the Jain Tirthankar Chintamani Parswanath and was for many years among the sights of Ahmadabad.

Shantidas's temple at Saraspur (a suburb to the east of Ahmadabad) was unfortunately destined to pass through unhappy vicissitudes. Mandelslo visited it in 1638, only seven years before it received its fatal blow. In 1645–6 Prince Aurangzeb was appointed viceroy of Gujarat by his father Shah Jahan, and his religious bigotry, which was manifest at this early age, led him to desecrate this beautiful shrine. According to Thevenot (1666) he caused a cow to be killed in the place and then converted it into a mosque, destroying at the same time the noses of all the figures in the temple. The author of the *Mirat-i-Ahmadi* says that the mosque received from the prince the name of *Quvvat-ul-Islam* (the Might of Islam).

Shantidas may perhaps have complained about this sacrilege to the court of Shah Jahan, where his influence was most powerful. The result was the issue of a *farman* by the emperor, dated 1648, addressed to the imperial governor and officials at Ahmadabad, to the effect that a wall should be raised between the *mihrabs* constructed by Prince Aurangzeb and the rest of the temple and that the building should again be handed over to Shantidas for the conduct of worship according to his religion. Besides, the fakirs who had made their home in the building were to be removed and any materials that might have been carried away from the temple were to be restored. The original of this valuable *farman* was fifty years ago in the possession of the head of the Nagarsheth family at Ahmadabad, but now only an imperfect copy of it, made under the directions of the late A. Kinloch Forbes, is to be found among the manuscript records of the Forbes Gujarati Sabha at Bombay.

According to tradition, after the Moslem desecration, the principal images in the temple of Shantidas were brought over to the city through an underground tunnel, which was large enough for the passage of a cart, to the Jhaveriwada at Ahmadabad, and installed in other temples which were erected for them. This may be accepted without reserve for, in spite of Shah Jahan's *farman*, it was not likely that the devout Jains would again proceed to worship in a place which had been so desecrated by the Mogul prince. The language used by Thevenot, who visited the city in 1666, gives the impression that the building was no longer a Hindu shrine. We may conclude then that from the third quarter of the seventeenth century this magnificent structure began to fall into neglect on the part of Jains as well as Moslems. In the course of over 260 years that have elapsed since then, the temple has suffered not less from the deliberate spoliation of man than by the ravages of time. It is a matter of no small regret that while the magnificent Moslem monuments of the fifteenth and sixteenth centuries still remain in almost perfect condition, this temple of Shantidas, built in the seventeenth century, has practically disappeared.

APPENDIXES TO CHAPTER VII

(A) ACCOUNTS OF THE NEW COLLEGE OF ST. PAUL GIVEN BY P. DELLA VALLE AND DR. JOHN FRYER

The Italian traveller, P. Della Valle, who was at Goa in 1623, says:

'The Jesuits, I say, resolute to abide there, prevailing hitherto both against the City (which recalls them back to San Paolo Vecchio for greater convenience of the students) and against the Augustines, and against the King himself, who hath many times ordained their removal and the destruction of their new College, nevertheless maintain themselves in possession of their new and sumptuous fabric, which also they daily enlarge and nominate San Paolo Nuovo, for in India they will have all their colleges dedicated to St. Paul, the Doctor of the Gentiles.'—*Travels in India*, Hakluyt Society (1892) vol. II, p. 404.

The English surgeon Dr. John Fryer, who arrived at Goa during Christmas week 1675, says:

'The Paulistines (i.e. Jesuits) enjoy the biggest of all the monasteries at St. Roch; in it is a library, an hospital, and an apothecary's shop well furnished with medicines, where Gasper Antonio, a Florentine, a lay-brother of the Order, the author of the Goa stores, brings them in 50,000 xeraphins[1] by that invention annually: he is an old man, and almost blind, being of great esteem for his long practice in physic. It (the college) is built like a Cross and shows like a seraglio on

[1] The word xeraphin represents a silver coin, formerly current at Goa and other eastern ports, and worth about 1*s.* 5*d.* The term is here a corruption applied to a degenerated value. The original is the Arabic *ashrafi* (or *sharifi* = noble) which was applied to various gold coins, especially to the *dinar* of Egypt, and to the gold *mohur* of India.—cf. *Hobson-Jobson*.

the Water.'—Fryer, *East India and Persia*, Hakluyt Society (1909–12) vol. II, pp. 11–12.

(B) PYRARD DE LAVAL ON THE CHURCH OF BOM JESUS, 1608–9

'It was richly built and all gilded within; it is not yet complete, but the work is proceeding day by day. I have seen there a cross of solid gold, which the company of Jesuit Fathers have had made for a present to the Pope: it was three feet in length, four fingers in width, and two in thickness, and embellished with all manner of precious stones richly set: it was priced there at more than 100,000 crowns and was sent to His Holiness by the vessel on which I embarked on my return.' —*Voyage of Pyrard de Laval*, Hakluyt Society (1887) vol. II, p. 59.

(C) P. DELLA VALLE'S ACCOUNT OF THE CANONIZATION CEREMONIES OF ST. FRANCIS XAVIER AT GOA IN 1624

The elaborate ceremonies of the canonization began at Goa on 10 February 1624 and ended on 19 February, on which day the body of the saint was transferred with great pomp from St. Paul's to the Church of Bom Jesus. On the first day the Jesuits sang vespers in the Church of Bom Jesus and the same night there was a masquerade in which young students passed through the streets on horseback, clothed in rich dresses, and carrying a standard which portrayed the effigies of the saints. The next day (11th), after a solemn mass, a sermon was delivered in the same church by the Visitor, Andrea Palmeiro, at which the viceroy was present. A great theatre had been erected in the piazza outside the church, with seats all round both for men and women, in which was enacted for several days together the life of St. Francis Xavier. Here on the 12th, in presence of the viceroy, the nobility and the people, the first act of the 'Tragedy' was represented by some thirty persons, all richly clothed and decked with jewels, who staged the play with an elaborate machinery of 'chariots, ships, galleys, pageants,[1] heavens, hells, mountains and clouds'. The show depicted not only all the events of the saint's life, but also his death, the transport of his body to Goa, his ascent to heaven, and lastly his canonization by the Pope. On the 19th, which was the last day, a very solemn procession started from the Church of San Paolo Vecchio (old St. Paul's) and proceeded to that of Bom Jesus with pageant, chariots, ships and other 'brave devices'. At the rear of this procession several Jesuit fathers, dressed in their copes, carried the body of St. Francis Xavier enclosed in a fine and rich silver coffin with a silver canopy over it and the effigy of the saint behind. Then came a great standard bearing the effigies of the saints which was also carried by the Fathers. Then came all the crosses of the parishes in Salsette and lastly only one company of Franciscan friars. This fraternity, we are told, did not join the processions of the Jesuits because the latter did not attend theirs. With this ended the solemnities of the canonization. —*Travels of P. Della Valle*, Hakluyt Society (1892) vol. II, pp. 410–14.

(D) THE TOMB OF ST. FRANCIS XAVIER IN THE CHURCH OF BOM JESUS AT GOA

Neither Pyrard de Laval (1609) nor Pietro Della Valle (1623–4), nor Mandelslo (1639), nor Dr. Fryer (1675), nor Gemelli Careri (1695) saw the magnificent sarcophagus in the chapel of St. Francis Xavier in which the remains of the saint were enshrined soon after the visit of the last named traveller. According to the author of the *Oriente Conquistado* it was a gift from the Grand Duke of Tuscany in return for a pillow, on which the head of the saint reposed for many years after his death, which was presented to the Duke by the Provincial General of the Jesuits. The tomb, which is a very beautiful example of Florentine workmanship, is made of rich

[1] Pageant here means the movable structure or 'carriage', consisting of a stage and stage machinery, used in the open-air performances of the mystery plays.

jasper and the finest marbles of variegated colours, and consists of three tiers with plates or panels curiously wrought representing various incidents in the life of the saint. The whole is surmounted by the far-famed coffin, overlaid with silver. It has thirty-two panels in the same metal depicting in relief scenes from the saint's career, and with figures of angels supporting a beautiful cross two and a half feet high.

The body of the saint is still, after the lapse of nearly four centuries, in a well-preserved state, though it has shrunk to some extent, being only four and a half feet in length. The right arm is wanting, having been cut off by order of the Pope on 3 November 1614, and divided into four parts, the larger of which was sent to Rome. Two of the toes of the right foot are missing, one of them being bitten off in 1554, when being kissed by a Portuguese lady who was anxious to possess a relic of the saint. In 1556 a physician certified the body to be still free from corruption and to yield blood. The saint is clad in elegantly embroidered garments studded with pearls, the gift of Maria Sofia, wife of Dom Pedro II, King of Portugal, who made them about the year 1693. At the feet of the saint hangs a gold medallion with legends on both sides.

The body of the saint was formerly very frequently exposed for public veneration by the Jesuits who had charge of it. As late as Dr. Fryer's time (1675) this was done once a year, generally on the day of the festival of the saint (3 December). Some years before Gemelli's visit in 1695 this practice appears to have been stopped to prevent the danger of injury to the body by the populace who would be eager to secure some relic of the saint. Only the viceroy and a few other persons of quality were allowed to see it. Even this privilege was withdrawn by a royal letter dated 2 April 1755, and since then the body is shown only by express orders from the Government of Portugal. This exposition has taken place in 1782, 1859, 1878, 1910 and 1922. On all these occasions a vast concourse of people of all races and creeds from several parts of India assembled at Goa to honour the Apostle of the

Indies or to benefit by the miraculous cures which were believed to be effected by his intercession. The old city of Goa appeared on these occasions to have risen from its ruins and to have recovered the glory which it displayed nearly three centuries ago.—Fonseca, *Sketch of Goa*, pp. 290–300.

(E) PYRARD DE LAVAL'S ACCOUNT OF THE ROYAL HOSPITAL AT GOA

Pyrard de Laval, a Frenchman, was brought to Goa as a prisoner in 1608 and was treated in this hospital for three weeks. His account is the most detailed and exhaustive that is available to us about the internal administration of this famous institution. We give below extracts from the same.

'Viewing it from the outside we could hardly believe it was an hospital; it seemed to us a grand palace, saving the inscription above the gate: *Hospitale del Rey Nostro Seignoro* (p. 3) . . . . The beds are beautifully shaped and lacquered with red varnish; the sacking is of cotton; the mattresses and coverlets are of silk or cotton, adorned with different patterns (p. 4) . . . In the evening they brought us supper at the appointed hour, to each a large fowl roasted, with some dessert, so we were astonished at the good cheer we received (p. 5) . . . This hospital is, as I believe, the finest in the world, whether for the beauty of the building and its appurtenances, the accommodation being in all respects excellent, or for the perfect order, regulation and cleanliness observed, the great care taken of the sick, and the supply of all comforts that can be wished for (p. 5) . . . It is of very great extent, situated on the banks of the river, and endowed by the kings of Portugal with 25,000 perdos (i.e. over £5,000), let alone the endowments and presents which it receives from the lords. This is a large revenue for the purpose in those parts, seeing food is so cheap, and the management so good; for the Jesuits who carry it on send as far as Cambay and elsewhere for wheat, provisions, stuffs and all other necessaries (p. 6) . . . It is managed and governed by the Jesuits, who appoint a Father to the post of governor. The other officers are Portuguese, all men of quality and gentility; as for the servants and slaves, they are Christian Indians. The Jesuit Father is superior over all the rest, who are like the inmates of a large monastery, each having his own office (p. 6) . . . There are physicians, surgeons and apothecaries, barbers and bleeders, who do nothing else, and are bound to visit each of the sick twice a day. The apothecary is one of the household, and lives in the hospital, and has his shop well stocked at the hospital's expense (p. 6). . . . The sick are sometimes very numerous, and while I was there were as many as 1,500, all of them either Portuguese soldiers or men of other Christian races of Europe, of every profession and quality. Indians are not taken in there, having a hospital apart wherein are received only Christian Indians (p. 7) . . . Two Jesuits, and more if need be, are in attendance, who do nothing else but go round confessing and comforting the sick, administering the sacrament and giving them beads for saying their prayers (p. 11) . . . No women are allowed to enter, sick or sound. Nor are any householders received, neither men, women, nor children. This hospital is only for the *Soldades*, that is, for such as are not married or domiciled, but are soldiers of fortune (p. 12) . . . Sometimes they are visited by the archbishop, the viceroy, and many lords, who make gifts to them of large sums of money; and everyone takes pleasure in seeing so splendid a place, where all the rooms are clean and white as paper (p. 12).—*Voyage of Pyrard de Laval*, Hakluyt Society (1887) vol. II, pp. 3–15.

APPENDIX TO CHAPTER IX

WILLIAM BAYLEY'S ACCOUNT OF THE HOMEWARD VOYAGE OF THE 'MARY'[1]

It is interesting to compare the dates and incidents in Mandelslo's account of the voyage with those given in the log of the *Mary*, by William Bayley.[2] The two are in substantial agreement.

'January 5, 1639. Sailed. Met the *Michael*, which departed the same evening for Rajapur.

January 7, 1639. Anchored at Bassein, where they found the *Blessing*.

January 10, 1639. Anchored off Goa.

January 11, 1639. "This morning came aboard us the General and Vice-Admiral of the fleet, with divers other gentlemen from the fleet and city. About ten o'clock the President, etc., went ashore with the General, and so to the city of Goa, where they were kindly entertained."

January 22, 1639. Sailed for Cannanore, "to relieve those English captives as were of the *Comfort*, taken by the Malabars."

January 25, 1639. Anchored at Cannanore, where they found Captain Weddell.

January 26, 1639. Repaid Captain Weddell 2,200 rials of eight, which he had spent in redeeming the master and fourteen men of the *Comfort* from the Malabars.

January 30, 1639. Seventeen Malabar frigates attacked the *Mary*, but were repulsed.

February 4, 1639. Passed Cape Comorin.

March 21, 1639. Fire in the steward's room.

March 27, 1639. At a general consultation it was decided to make for Mauritius to wood and water.

[1] *Marine Records*, vol. lxii, p. 107.

[2] He was master or captain of the *Mary*.

March 28, 1639. Sighted Rodriguez. Another consultation held, at which it was unanimously decided to go direct to the Cape of Good Hope.

April 5, 1639. Passed Cape Sèbastian, on Madagascar.

April 28, 1639. Saw the African coast.

May 1, 1639. Cape Falso sighted.

May 5, 1639. Got into Table Bay.

May 11, 1639. Their boat carried twenty natives to Penguin Island, there to reside.

May 30, 1639. Having had extremely bad weather, in which the ship had suffered severely and had been beaten back from the Cape, it was determined to bear up for Madagascar.

June 3, 1639. The wind changing, they stood for the Cape once more.

June 10, 1639. After enduring another storm, and finding the vessel very leaky, it was resolved to make for Madagascar again.

June 24, 1639. Abraham Aldington fell overboard, but was saved.

June 28, 1639. Overtook the *William*, belonging to Courteen's Association and commanded by Edward Hall.

July 3, 1639. Anchored in St. Augustine's Bay, and found there the *London*, under Captain Wills, bound for Surat.

August 21, 1639. The *Mary* sailed for England.

September 14, 1639. They estimated that they had doubled the Cape.

October 9, 1639. Thought they saw St. Helena, but, finding that they had shot past the island, they resumed the voyage.

October 19, 1639. Crossed the Line.

November 7, 1639. Joseph, an Italian passenger, was put in irons for wounding Emanuel Fonseca, a Portuguese.

November 29, 1639. Sighted some of the Azores.

December 16, 1639. Anchored in the Downs.

December 21, 1639. Methwold " went away for London ".

December 26, 27, 1639. A severe storm.'

—*English Factories in India* (1637-41) edited by Foster, pp. 120-22.

INDEX